I0795049

COLUMBUS AND THE GREAT FLOOD OF 1913

COLUMBUS AND THE GREAT FLOOD OF 1913

THE DISASTER THAT RESHAPED THE OHIO VALLEY

CONRADE C. HINDS

THE History PRESS

Published by The History Press
Charleston, SC 29403
www.historypress.net

First published 2013

Manufactured in the United States

ISBN 978.1.62619.061.0

Library of Congress CIP data applied for.

Notice: The information in this book is true and complete to the best of our knowledge. It is offered without guarantee on the part of the author or The History Press. The author and The History Press disclaim all liability in connection with the use of this book.

Dana Avenue Elementary School opened for the 1912–13 school year. *CPS.*

This book is especially dedicated to the lifetime spirit of learning and sanctuary at the Dana Avenue Elementary School of Columbus' Franklinton area. In addition to being a flood survivor and a fortified castle of early education for six generations of Columbus children, the physical building served as one of many refuge and relief stations for hundreds of people who instantly lost their homes to floodwater when the south bank levee of the Scioto River broke on March 24, 1913. The swift-flowing water penetrated the lower levels of the building, but the masonry and concrete foundations held firm. They did not give way to the pounding they received from the muddy flood currents and nearly endless debris. Today, a plaque is mounted on the wall of the main floor corridor that indicates the point near the ceiling where the floodwater crested above the floor inside the building. Unfortunately, when the flood was over, twelve neighborhood children who attended Dana Avenue were counted with the casualties. The Dana Avenue Elementary School is a profound Columbus landmark not because of the age of its bricks and mortar but because of the lives that the structure has helped save, shape and foster. This building even stands as the birthplace of a baby during the 1913 flood. The mother named her Dana Rose because the school gave the expecting mother comfort and security when she had no other place to lay her head. Baby Dana Rose was born in room 11 according to the school's register book. It is a story such as this that, if remembered and consistently retold, breathes a meaning of life into the elementary school that sustains the community's hope and confidence to stand and accept future challenges. Dana Avenue Elementary School is a Columbus landmark that has stayed constant, evolving from blackboards when the school first opened its doors in 1912 to the current Smart Boards.

Contents

Preface 9
Acknowledgements 11
Introduction 13

The Gamble of Living the Good Life in the Flood Plain 17
An Alaskan Volcanic Winter at Our Front Door 24
The "What" and "Why" of Floods and Flooding 29
Ohio Flood History 33
Twentieth-Century Flooding Puts on a Different Face 41
Enter the Grand Champion of Ohio Floods 45
West Columbus Caught by Surprise 50
The Local Fear of a Dam Break 83
Statewide Communication Failure and Restoration 90
Wheeling, West Virginia, and Zanesville, Ohio 99
Chillicothe and Dayton 105
A Plan of Solutions and Opposition to Common Sense 118

Epilogue: The Test of Readiness and Lessons Learned 129
Appendix: Significant Events that Shaped the World of 1912–1913 141
Bibliography 149
Index 153
About the Author 157

Preface

In writing this book about the 1913 flood, I hope to spotlight attention to another event that served to shape the Columbus metropolitan community and much of Ohio as we know it today. If a first-time visitor to Columbus looked at the civic improvements along the downtown Scioto River waterfront, they would be amazed. Why? Because for a city not widely known for having a grand downtown waterway like San Antonio's Paseo del Rio river walk, Columbus has made improvements along the banks of the Scioto that inspire a feeling of awe. Two landmarks that stand out as unique are the full-scale replica of Christopher Columbus's *Santa Maria* ship on the east bank and the larger-than-life Columbus Museum of Science and Industry on the west bank. Both sites are positioned very well in relation to the river and the main east–west thoroughfare crossing the river, the Broad Street Bridge. The main event of the twentieth century that ties all three of these landmarks together is the March 1913 flood. The flood was not as destructive as the 1971 Chicago Fire, but to Columbus and many other Ohio Valley cities, it was just as influential in its impact on future development.

I would like to give Columbus and Ohio a look at what has created our community and culture beyond the daily low expectations of faddish fast food, football and video games. This is not just another look at a natural disaster. Instead, it highlights how Ohioans have traditionally approached disasters, not as victims but as problem solvers.

Acknowledgements

Ohio wasn't built by America, but it is my opinion that America was built by Ohio's broad application of its profound innovative spirit, and for that I am very grateful.

Thank you to Tom Betti and Doreen Uhas Sauer for extending an invitation to participate in writing a book for the Columbus Landmarks Foundation history book series and to my wife, Dr. Janet L. Hinds, for her help in scholarly research and generous sharing. Thanks to the Education Committee of the Columbus Landmarks Foundation for its insight and creativity. A note of gratitude goes to Eleanor Walters, Marshall Hinds, Roger C. Huff, Jack and Linda Solt, William Poteet, Kris Akins, Alexander Malone, Al Manning, Ray Harpham, Don Barnes, Al Wansing and the late Doug Brookhart for all their positive encouragement, help and patience, as well as for opening the doors of opportunity for me over the past forty or more years. And my continued thanks go to those who support preserving the Columbus community and Ohio heritage as an international leader of innovation, invention and civic problem solving.

Special thanks to my late parents and grandparents, Dr. Conrade and Ada Hinds and Russell and Ethel Davidson, respectively, and Minerva Saddler for sharing their insight and wisdom. I'd also like to extend my deepest warm acknowledgement to Charles Rinehart for his confidence in me as an educator. I give my grateful appreciation to John Sauer for his constructive editing and to Bill Mattes, Ed Lentz and the Board of Columbus Landmarks Foundation for their support, as well as the ever-creative Education

Committee. And finally, a gracious thank-you goes to Sandy Andromeda of the Franklinton Historical Society and Joe Gartrell of The History Press.

Photo credits include image from Columbus Metropolitan Library Image Collections (CML), Columbus Public Schools (CPS), *Columbus Dispatch* (CD), Conrade Hinds Collection (CH), private collection (PC), Ohio Historic Society (OHS), Columbus Division of Water (CDW), Library of Congress (LOC) and Wright State University Libraries, Special Collections and Archives (WSUL).

Introduction

Often we hear and see how a community rallies the very best of human nature and puts it into diligent practice during times of natural disasters. This is because disasters force humans to focus on the first priority of life: to survive. Progress is generally achieved rapidly when people using common sense to quickly discern that the odds of survival increase through mutual cooperation. But for those who feel routinely disenfranchised, such as a number of urban citizens during the aftermath of Hurricane Katrina, their only thoughts of surviving may be through taking advantage of others by looting, demonstrating classic dog-eat-dog behavior. This is probably because they normally exist in an at-risk social environment with very little mutual cooperation. Given this, a natural disaster is only a catalyst to more self-centered preservation behavior. Surviving the 1913 flood throughout the Midwest routinely meant opening one's mind to helping and being helped by others. For many, this even took the shape of the ultimate sacrifice when people gave their lives in an effort to rescue others.

The Great Flood of 1913 was so named because it affected everyone, not only in Ohio but also throughout the entire Midwest region of the United States and beyond. This single event did much to reshape the general look of most midsize and large cities of the Midwest. Historically, flooding has been the supreme disaster that has repeatedly unleashed its fury on the state of Ohio. And yet despite a variety of public works and engineering marvels, flooding still remains a serious threat to the general welfare of much of the state's population. Each year, this state endures destructive runs of high

A group of local west side Columbus kids looking amazed and bewildered at the sight of their neighborhood and the Scioto River flood destruction in this drawing by artist Billy Ireland for the *Columbus Evening Dispatch*. *CD.*

water that wreak havoc on the lives of the innocent victims of these natural weather occurrences. Early settlers established homes and farms on and near bottomland flood plains adjacent to rivers and their associated tributaries because of the rich productive soil and their proximity to a supply of water for irrigation and transportation. About eighteen severe floods and more than thirty lesser floods, along with a sizable number of local floods, have taken place in Ohio over the past 250 years. Severe floods are generally caused by excessive river flow or infrastructure failures such as a dam break, and a minor flood may just be an event related to local rainfall. These floods have distressed thousands, claimed hundreds of lives and resulted in property damage in the billions of dollars based on today's property values.

Over the decades following the record-breaking flood of 1913, much has been written chronicling the resulting devastation and the human misery that was inflicted on a number of communities in the Midwest Ohio Valley. For this reason, it is prudent at this time—which marks the centennial of the region's worst natural disaster—to take a closer look at the intrinsic nature of floods and the reasons that civilizations are repeatedly affected by such events. Natural disasters are events in which man somehow gets in the way of the general seasonal function of the earth as a living environment for many diverse forms of life. It has long been the attitude of mankind to use the earth strictly for immediate needs, wants and gratification, without an understanding or acceptance of how the earth is able to generate the bounty that is beneficial to us. Unlike most living creatures and inhabitants on earth, man has survived by forcing nature's compliance, while most creatures adapt themselves to the restraints of nature and therefore live in harmony with their natural environment.

Floods are caused by numerous environmental, seasonal and human factors. All flooding can be dangerous and potentially deadly, although infrastructure and property damage are among the most common outcomes. Large-scale floods are generally thought of as the most dangerous, but smaller floods and flash floods can also cause significant harm. It takes as little as two feet of running floodwater to sweep away a large vehicle or drown a person caught up in its currents. During the 1913 flood, death came when levees broke and sent a tsunami-like flash flood of water sweeping into unsuspecting neighborhoods throughout the Ohio Valley and beyond.

The Gamble of Living the Good Life in the Flood Plain

Flood disasters are the result of a curious love-hate relationship between human beings and their tendency to not just work but also live in flood plains. In some cases, such as New Orleans, people have even chosen to live below sea level—without the savvy heritage like the Dutch for draining coastal areas and properly constructing and maintaining dams and levees. Taking into account all the natural hazards that occur in the world, flooding is the most universal. For millennia, floods have been responsible for more deaths and caused more damage than any other form of natural disaster.

The term "flood" is used to describe water overflowing onto a landmass that is generally regarded as a dry area. Floods are classified in a variety of ways, starting with the common coastal and river floods and leading to the flooding of urban areas and inland flooding. There are also horrific floods that are results of typhoons or hurricanes, as well as sudden flash flooding. Each one of these floods has its own distinctive causes for development and unique characteristics; all can be dangerous, though, and flooding can occur anywhere, even in a desert.

Over the millennia of human history, people have established communities adjacent to ocean coasts and inland rivers for the most obvious reasons, as well as to be near a source of water and food. Access to a fresh water supply that was used for drinking and cooking was essential to the general well-being of communities large or small. In a number of towns, water was the primary power source, used to operate equipment such as the gears and wheel of a mill for grinding corn and wheat grain. A strong, continuous flow of water is also used to operate large hydroelectric power generators.

Another advantage to establishing business and industry close to water was that it proved an efficient route by which to travel and transport large cargos of agricultural comities and, later, industrial goods. But the undisputed disadvantage of living near a body of water is the possibility and, in many cases, the certainty of flooding.

The planet contains the same amount of water as it had during the age of dinosaurs, and the amount of water on Earth at any given time remains fairly constant. As a result of what is known as the hydrologic cycle, a small amount of the earth's surface water routinely evaporates into the atmosphere. At a very slow rate, the surface water of the rivers, lakes and oceans continually evaporates. About 97 percent of the water on the earth is in the physical form of liquid and is salt water. Near the North and South Poles, we find water in a solid form as glacier ice, and these masses account for an additional 2 percent of Earth's water. Surprisingly, less than 1 percent of the water is fresh water, and that is mostly contained as groundwater, which is extracted from a well or underground spring.

Looking closer at the effect of the hydrologic cycle and how it affects flooding, we see large amounts of water vapor in the air as a result of evaporation from the surface of bodies of water. Curiously, these water molecules remain adrift in the atmosphere for an estimated nine to ten days before falling as rain or snow. This occurs because the water vapor in a cloud condenses and starts to form drops of water, which then descend to earth. The rainwater completes the hydrologic cycle by returning to the earth and various bodies of water. The full cycle then begins again. The rain that soaks into the ground will spend a period of time as groundwater.

In the American Midwest, river flooding is the most common type of flooding, and the rivers are where a vast majority of the population is found. It is often the Midwest experience for flooding to occur when the annual rainfall is very unevenly distributed. Far too much rain flows as runoff into the river at one time, and the amount of water greatly exceeds the capacity of the river channel. When this occurs, a stream will naturally overflow its banks. Another frequent cause of river flooding is rapidly melting snow in the spring. When snow melts in regions that have hills or mountains, the water quickly flows down into the streams and estuaries until the water arrives at the river. If the snowfall was heavier than usual, floods may occur because spring rains often occur simultaneously with the snowmelt, contributing more water to the streams and rivers. Also, the land is often already saturated to its maximum level.

In October 2012, the torrential rains that accompanied Hurricane Sandy served as a prime example of how a tropical storm can also cause flooding in the Midwest region of the United States. Mud is formed when heavy rains fall on bare soil, and this condition keeps the runoff water from soaking into the ground. The majority of the runoff will flow over the surface of the ground, causing gully erosion that will carry most of the runoff to the rivers and streams.

Particularly in the Ohio Valley, areas of land near bodies of water such as rivers and lakes and land at lower elevations relative to the surrounding terrain are highly susceptible to flooding. When the water rises beyond its safe level, it will generally flow over its banks or shores and into adjacent areas. Naturally, the water will settle at the lowest possible point and will, as a result, flood any areas that are at or below the current water level. In areas where the ground is not dry, nonporous or otherwise incapable of absorbing water because of oversaturation, flooding will occur as a result of sudden or seasonal rains. Such a condition was one of the primary causes of the 1913 Easter weekend flooding that devastated the Ohio Valley. An enormous set of storms and peculiar weather patterns caused significant flooding in major Ohio cities such as Columbus, Dayton, Zanesville, Chillicothe and Cincinnati and as far away as Louisville, Kentucky, and Indianapolis, Indiana.

In Ohio, dams are often used for flood control in addition to providing a public water supply. When such structures are erected at the headwaters of the stream, they are frequently engineered to withstand and retain heavy runoff, and the water is then released gradually to flow to a treatment facility during dry periods and droughts. Floodways are another means of controlling floodwater. This practice diverts floodwater into a controlled area to prevent the flooding of other areas. Planting trees to reestablish forests significantly helps in areas where flooding occurs because of deforestation and soil erosion.

Floods can be extremely deadly and should not be taken lightly as just a routine springtime phenomenon. So far as death toll is concerned, the worst flood in the United States was the 1889 Johnstown, Pennsylvania flood. Johnstown was an industrial steel town unfortunately built in the floodplain and located at the fork of the Little Conemaugh and Stony Creek Rivers. To guard against flooding, the community constructed an earthen dam on the Little Conemaugh River some fourteen miles upstream from the town. The

The Cincinnati downtown business district at high water during the flood. For months afterward, various establishments had a mildew smell as they continued to dry out. *LOC.*

The Johnstown, Pennsylvania Flood of 1889. Piles of debris are being removed from a stone bridge. Columbus citizens still remembered that nearly two thousand people died during this flood that was the result of a dam break. *LOC.*

South Fork Dam, as it was known, formed and held back a lake about three miles in length and bordered by a mountain 450 feet higher than Johnstown. Like many earthen dams, the South Fork had been poorly maintained, and on the afternoon of May 31, 1889, following several days of extremely heavy rainfall and a torrential rain the previous night, Johnstown residents were startled by a roar that sounded like thunder. Some immediately realized that the dam had broken.

The dam's failure unleashed a torrent of 20 million tons of water (equaling 4.8 billion U.S. gallons) that was making its way down the narrow valley to Johnstown. The wall of muddy water and debris periodically exceeded sixty feet in height and leveled everything in its path. As thousands of people scrambled, trying to get out of the way of the water, many were engulfed and swept downstream along with the debris. A number of fortunate people made their way downstream to the old Stone Bridge, where the two rivers met, by clinging to debris that served as rafts. However, much of the debris caught fire when it hit the bridge because of kerosene fuel from lanterns and sparks from metal raking over the rocks. At least eighty people who had managed to cling to something as they were swept downstream died in the fire. Many of the missing were never found, and many bodies could not be identified. The cleanup took years, and bodies were found for months after the flood.

The Johnstown flood had a volumetric flow rate that temporarily equaled that of the average flow rate of the Mississippi River, but in a greatly confined area. By all accounts, the entire flood killed 2,209 people and could have been avoided if better attention had been given to maintaining the South Fork Dam, which was built primarily for flood control. In this respect, the Johnstown flood wasn't a natural disaster but rather an event made disastrous because of man's lack of priorities, appreciation of maintenance and respect for the power of nature. Flooding is a common event in nature, but by factoring in human decisions that are so often more akin to gambles, we set the stage for nature being paired with a human disaster rooted in negligence.

The scope of flood deaths and destruction in the entire United States is relatively minor. To quickly gain a heightened respect for the power of nature regarding floods, we need only look at the flooding in other parts of the world, such as in China. Along the Yellow (Huang He) River in China, flooding has historically killed more people than at any other river or waterway in the world. It is estimated that about 2 million people died in the flood of 1887. Looking at the twentieth century alone, nearly 4 million people were killed by a flood in 1931, and in 1938, there were almost 1 million casualties. The death toll of those three floods together is nearly equal to the human carnage of the Jewish holocaust during World War II. The channel of the river is choked by millions of tons of silt and mud, and this causes the river to overflow its banks quite often and redirect its course. In many areas, the riverbed is at a higher elevation than the surrounding countryside. Although dikes as high as thirty feet have been constructed, they periodically fail to hold back the water.

For centuries, the Chinese have tried to control the river by building numerous levees and dams and excavating drainage channels. In recent times, the Chinese people hope to be on their way to finally alleviating their problems of flooding along the Yellow River with the construction of a massive capital improvement called the Xiaolangdi Multipurpose Dam Project. It is located at the last gorge of the middle reach of the Yellow River. The main purpose of the project is flood control, in addition to ice jam control, sediment control, irrigation, water supply and generation of hydroelectric power. The project consists of many structures, including ten intake towers, nine flood and sediment tunnels and an earth-and rock-filled dam with a sloping impervious core. Xiaolangdi is located in a key position for flood and sediment control of the Yellow River. Upon completion, the Xiaolangdi Dam and Reservoir will effectively mitigate catastrophic flooding, and the control level of the river will be increased from the present less-than-one-hundred-year-return period to ten thousand years. Also, it will reduce the severe flooding of the flood plain of the lower regions. Such development doesn't occur without criticism from the western developed countries regarding resettlement and environmental impact issues. During this critique, the human death toll of previous floods is often overlooked.

Elsewhere in the world, the Nile River floods like clockwork every summer. For many centuries, the Egyptians took advantage of the fertile soil deposited during the flooding. Recently, though, they have been forced to grow more crops to feed their growing population. In the 1960s, Egypt constructed the Aswan High Dam across the Nile six hundred miles south of Cairo, the Egyptian capital. This dam curtailed the annual flooding by retaining the water in a reservoir and then gradually releasing this water for use during the dry season. These flood control measures expanded the growing season because local farmers no longer needed to wait for the annual floodwater to recede before mobilizing to plant their crops. At first sight, it would appear that man and nature were now working in equilibrium. However, without the annual flooding to nourish the soil, the land is no longer as fertile as it had been prior to the dam installation. Consequently, farmers must now use large amounts of fertilizer to produce an acceptable yield.

Closer to home, the Mississippi River, like the Yellow River in China, regularly flooded its banks for thousands of years. An often-overlooked disastrous flood in 1927 killed 246 people in seven states. It flooded 16,570,627 acres and caused more than $400 million in damage (in today's money). This event prompted the federal government to initiate measures to gain more control of the river. The U.S. Army Corps of Engineers went to work constructing the longest levee system ever conceived in history. This massive project on the Mississippi incorporates twenty-nine locks and dams in addition to a multiple-state levee system and hundreds of runoff drainage channels. In general, this system operates quite well. However, in 1993, while most of the federal levees held firm, 80 percent of the private and municipal earthen levees along the river failed. As a result, torrents of river water rushed out onto fields and into the adjacent communities and towns.

Flooding has proved to be more deadly and disastrous in less developed regions of the world for two very obvious reasons. First, there is either very marginal or no flood control in most underdeveloped countries. Second, the government leadership fails to establish an early warning or emergency response system for the benefit of the general public. Flooding in North America kills far fewer people today than it did one hundred years ago because of these advances. Early warning systems have proven to be effective and efficient, and meteorological technology such as radar has advanced our ability to better predict floods. Almost everyone has access to electronic media such as radio or television and can quickly be advised of an imminent flood in time to take safety measures. Most communities have disaster mobilization plans that designate several evacuation routes to be used in the event of a flood. Flood control public works facilities that include levees, dams, runoff drainage channels and breakwaters have been constructed over the years and make it unlikely that a flood of the magnitude of the Johnstown flood, 1913 Ohio Valley flood or the 1927 flood on the Mississippi will occur again.

An Alaskan Volcanic Winter at Our Front Door

It has only been in the past few decades that the American general public has started to get a real understanding of how natural and climatic events elsewhere in the world can and do affect them and their general well-being. Yet many still view global warming as a myth conjured up by tree-hugging environmentalist liberals. But documented scientific facts clearly illustrate that the world's weather patterns have changed over the past half a dozen decades. Our oceans are rising and glaciers are melting. In regard to the 1913 flood, the subject of changing weather patterns can be raised by asking a simple question: how did a volcanic eruption in the Alaskan territory the previous year contribute to the conditions that caused tremendous flooding in the Ohio Valley in 1913? Today, we must ask whether this flood was a severe weather event with a one-hundred-year cycle and if we are prepared for an inevitable reoccurrence. Since there will be renewed focus and questions arising during the 2013 centennial year of this great flood, this is an avenue to gain new insight into this extreme event.

How can a flood in Midwestern America occur as a result of a volcanic eruption? It is possible that such an event could be initiated by a phenomenon known as a volcanic winter. A volcanic winter is the reduction in temperature resulting from volcanic ash and small drops of sulfuric acid that obscure the sun and raise the earth's albedo (an increase in the earth's reflectivity of solar radiation) following an extremely massive volcanic eruption. The eruption sends a massive amount of volcanic ash and sulfur aerosols into the upper stratosphere. The volcanic ash will decrease regional visibility for several months after the eruption, but the sulfur compounds injected into the stratosphere form sulfur aerosols that can reflect a portion of incoming sunlight for several years. As the concentration of sulfur aerosols increases in this level of the atmosphere, greater reflection occurs. Surface heating declines as a result, and thus cooler temperatures will prevail over the earth's surface. Compared with the lower, dense part of the atmosphere (the troposphere), the stratosphere is relatively devoid of any atmospheric turbulence. Given this condition, the suspended aerosols may remain in the stratosphere for several years before finally settling out. If sulfur aerosol loading is significant enough, it can initiate climate changes on a global scale for years following the event, triggering agricultural crop failures, temperature reduction and unusual weather conditions across the earth's surface.

For decades, experts believed that a climate calamity that occurred in AD 535–536 was due to a comet or asteroid hitting the earth. Today, though, it is widely thought that the event was probably the result of the most massive volcanic eruption of the past 1,500 years. This eruption threw so much sulfur dioxide gas into the stratosphere that a "volcanic winter" resulted due to the reduced amount of incoming sunlight. The eruption that led to the AD 535–536 climate calamity would have likely been a "super colossal" magnitude 7 event on the Volcanic Explosivity Index (VEI). An eruption of this magnitude is expected to occur only once every 1,000 years.

The Volcanic Explosivity Index is a logarithmic scale, like the Richter scale used to rate earthquakes. Specifically, a magnitude 7 eruption would eject ten times more material than either of the two largest eruptions of the past century. These two events were the magnitude 6 eruptions of Mount Pinatubo in the Philippines in 1991 and Novarupta in Alaska in June 1912. Given this understanding, the cause of the 1913 flood can, in part, be attributed to the 1912 eruption of Mount Katmai and its daughter volcano, Novarupta, in Alaska. In one of the greatest recorded volcanic events, Novarupta emitted enough fine ash into the atmosphere to block sunlight and cool the climate of the Northern Hemisphere that winter. For this reason, the idea of the volcanic winter can be associated with this event.

Novarupta, one of a chain of volcanoes on the Alaska Peninsula, erupted in June 1912. This was the largest volcanic eruption of the twentieth century, and it happened on Mount Katmai. A new volcano, also called Novarupta, formed as a result. The initial eruption actually took place at the Novarupta Volcano. Novarupta expelled magma and ash into the air that fell to earth and covered an area of 3,000 square miles more than 1 foot deep. During the eruption, the withdrawal of magma beneath Katmai resulted in the collapse

The 1912 eruption of the Novarupta Volcano in Alaska caused the volcanic winter conditions that were the catalyst of the Great Flood of 1913 in the Midwest. *LOC.*

of its summit area and formed a two-thousand-foot-deep caldera. The sixty-hour-long eruption expelled 3.1 to 3.6 cubic miles of magma, thirty times as much as Mount St. Helens in Washington State produced when it erupted in 1980. Additionally, the eruption resulted in about 2.6 cubic miles of ash flow, ending with the extrusion of a lava dome that plugged the vent. The 295-foot-high, 1,180-foot-wide dome, and the caldera it created, formed the Novarupta Volcano.

The planet's climate, thought to be normal by man's standards, changed considerably in 1912. Since the Industrial Revolution, the planet has experienced a greater than normal impact in climate change and global warming at the hands of humans. However, a variety of natural events also contribute to global warning. Some of the interesting related events include increased solar activity, earthquakes, asteroid impact, routine cyclical warming and cooling, regularly occurring North/South Pole shifts every several hundred (or even several thousand of years), algae accumulation in the oceans and even vegetation overeating by wildlife.

Over the millennia, animals and humans have migrated in order to find more suitable climates and food sources. This undoubtedly occurred before the Big Ice Age and still occurs today. If animals and people eat an area of land bare to the soil and move on, that soil turns into a desert. The land erodes with the rains and the winds, as shown most recently in America during the central region Dust Bowl in the 1930s. If this process were to

This picture of the Katmai Volcano eruption was actually taken in 1912 from a distance half a mile away. *LOC.*

remain constant for about one hundred years and cover the earth with deserts, the result would be the complete loss of our atmosphere, because plant life is necessary to sustain an atmosphere. The moon is a desert, and Mars is a cold desert. Their craters may be from volcanic activity in the past, as well as from more recent asteroid impacts. Volcanic activity can kill plants, wildlife and humans and drastically change the climate. This is what happened in Alaska in 1912.

Thunderstorms generally develop in warm, moist air in advance of eastward-moving cold fronts. These thunderstorms often produce large hail, strong winds and tornados. Tornados in the late winter and early spring are often associated with strong frontal systems that form in the central states and move east. In addition to floods being a product of torrential rains, tornados are formed in unusually violent thunderstorms when there is sufficient instability and wind shear present in the lower atmosphere. The term "instability" refers to the unusually warm and humid conditions in the lower atmosphere, as well as the possible presence of cooler than usual conditions in the upper atmosphere. Wind shear, in this case, refers to the wind direction changing and the wind speed increasing with height. An example would be a southerly wind of fifteen miles per hour at the surface changing to a southwesterly or westerly wind of fifty miles per hour at five thousand feet altitude. This kind of wind shear and instability usually exists only ahead of a cold front and low-pressure system. The intense spinning of a tornado is partly the result of the updrafts and downdrafts in the thunderstorm (caused by the unstable air) interacting with the wind shear, causing a tilting of the wind shear to form an upright tornado vortex.

Also adding to the process is the cyclonically flowing air around the cyclone, already slowly spinning in a counterclockwise direction (in the Northern Hemisphere), converging inward toward the thunderstorm and causing it to spin faster. This is the same process that causes ice skaters to spin faster when they pull their arms in toward their bodies.

Other processes can enhance the chances for tornado formation. For instance, dry air in the middle atmosphere can be rapidly cooled by rain in the thunderstorm, strengthening the downdrafts that are needed for tornado formation. Notice that in virtually every picture you see of a tornado, the tornado has formed on the boundary between dark clouds (the storm updraft region) and bright clouds (the storm downdraft region), evidence of the importance of updrafts and downdrafts to tornado formation. It is interesting that the 1913 flood caused most of its havoc during the first week of spring in a multi-state region of the United States that is historically known as "Tornado Alley."

The "What" and "Why" of Floods and Flooding

Many regard the super flood of 1913 as being a one-hundred-year flood. However, instead of using the phrase "one-hundred-year flood," most hydrologists prefer to describe these extreme hydrologic events as a flood having a one-hundred-year recurrence interval or cycle. What this specifically means will be described in detail in this chapter, but the simplest explanation is that, according to historical data about rainfall and stream stage, the probability of a typical river reaching a water elevation of twenty feet is once every one hundred years. This also means that a flood of that magnitude has a 1 percent chance of happening during any given year.

What exactly is meant by the phrase "recurrence interval"? If we incorporate statistical techniques by using a process called frequency analysis, we can estimate the probability of the occurrence of a given precipitation event. So, a recurrence interval can be based on the probability that the given event will be equaled or exceeded in any given year. An example of this would be to assume there is a one in fifty chance that 4.5 inches of rain will fall in a certain area in a twenty-four-hour period during any given year. Consequently, a rainfall total of 4.5 inches in a consecutive twenty-four-hour period is said to have a fifty-year recurrence interval. A rainfall recurrence interval is based on both the magnitude and the duration of a particular rainfall event, whereas a stream flow recurrence interval is based solely on the magnitude of the annual peak flow.

Ten or more years of data are required to perform a frequency analysis for the determination of recurrence intervals. It should be noted that the more years of historical data the better. This is because a professional hydrologist will have more confidence in an analysis of a river with thirty years of recorded data than one based on only ten years of record data.

Recurrence intervals for the annual peak stream flow at a given location change if there are significant changes in the flow patterns at that location, possibly caused by an impoundment or diversion of flow. The development and conversion of land from agricultural or forest uses to commercial, residential or industrial uses has a significant impact on peak flows. This impact is generally much greater for low-recurrence interval floods than for high-recurrence interval floods, such as twenty-five-, fifty- or one-hundred-year floods. During a larger flood, the soil is saturated to its limit and no longer has the capacity to absorb additional rainfall. Under these conditions, essentially all of the rain that falls, whether on paved surfaces or on saturated soil, will run off and add to the stream flow. These were the circumstances that compounded the flooding in the Ohio Valley in 1913.

It should be noted that a one-hundred-year storm does not always result in a one-hundred-year flood because of a number of factors that independently influence the cause-and-effect relation between rainfall and stream flow, such as the extent of rainfall on a land area that drains into a particular lake or river. This land area is referred to as a "watershed." In this case, when rainfall data are collected at a point within a stream basin, it is highly unlikely that this same amount of rainfall occurred uniformly throughout the entire basin. Especially during intensely localized storms, rainfall amounts throughout the basin can differ greatly from the rainfall amount measured at the location of the rain gauge. It is also not uncommon that some parts of the basin may even remain dry, supplying no additional runoff to the stream flow and lessening the impact of the storm.

Another factor mentioned earlier is the soil saturation prior to the storm. The existing condition of the soil before a given storm event will greatly influence the amount of storm water runoff into the stream system. Dry soil allows greater infiltration of rainfall and reduces the amount of runoff entering the stream. Conversely, soil that is already wet from previous rains has a lower capacity for infiltration, allowing more runoff to enter the stream. In the case of the 1913 Ohio Valley flood, the ground was still frozen due to a late winter, so the magnitude of runoff was tremendous.

The relation between the size of the watershed or stream basin and duration of the storm is another key factor to consider. It is easy to understand that a one-hundred-year storm with the duration of one hour in a five-square-mile watershed will have a more massive effect on the stream flow than the same storm in a fifty-square-mile watershed. This is because a stream with larger drainage area will require a rainstorm of longer duration for a significant increase in stream flow to occur. These are some of the major factors that determine whether or not a one-hundred-year storm will produce a one-hundred-year flood.

Next, we ask, what is the serious probability that a one-hundred-year flood will happen? Science tells us that there is approximately a 63.4 percent chance of one or more one-hundred-year floods occurring in any one-hundred-year period, not a 100 percent chance. In civil engineering, the field of extreme value theory was created to model rare events such as one-hundred-year floods. This theory is most commonly applied to the maximum or minimum observed stream flows of a given river. In desert areas where there are only ephemeral washes, this method is applied to the maximum observed rainfall over a given period of time (twenty-four hours, six hours or three hours). The extreme value analysis only considers the most extreme event observed in a given year. This means that between a large spring runoff and a heavy summer rainstorm, whichever produced the most water runoff would be considered the extreme event. The runoff of the smaller event would be ignored in the analysis, even though both may have been capable of causing terrible flooding in their own right.

Flooding is also determined by certain upstream factors that include the amount, location and timing required for water reaching a drainage channel that will determine the character of flowing water at a downstream location. The upstream water could start as natural precipitation or it could begin as a controlled or uncontrolled release from a supply reservoir. A small portion of the water will naturally evaporate, another portion will slowly percolate through the soil and some will be temporarily sequestered as snow or ice. Spring floods are often the result of rapid runoff from surfaces, including rock, pavement, roofs and saturated or frozen fields. The fraction of incident precipitation promptly reaching a drainage channel has been observed as being almost nothing for light rain on dry level ground and as high as 170 percent for warm rain on accumulated snow or frozen ground. This is because the warm rain melts the snow, thus adding to the amount of runoff. Columbus and the Ohio Valley experienced the latter in late March 1913.

Most precipitation records are based on a measured depth of water received within a fixed time interval. Convective precipitation events (thunderstorms) tend to produce shorter-duration storm events than orographic precipitation, which is a storm that occurs when moist air is lifted as it moves over a landmass such as a mountain range. As the air rises and cools, orographic clouds form and serve as the source of the precipitation, most of which falls upwind of the mountain ridge. Duration, intensity and frequency of rainfall events are important to flood prediction. Short-duration precipitation is more significant to flooding within small watersheds.

The most important upstream factor in determining floodwater quantity is the land area of the watershed upstream of the area that will flood. The duration and amount of rainfall are the second-most important factors for watersheds of less than thirty square miles, but the slope of the main drainage channel is the next most important factor for larger watersheds. Water flowing downhill ultimately encounters downstream conditions that reduce water movement. The final limitation is often a natural or artificial lake, as in the case of flood control dams and reservoirs. Elevation of flowing water is controlled by the simple geometry of the flow channel itself. Flow channel restrictions like bridges tend to control water elevation above the restriction. We must not forget that effective flood channel geometry may also be changed by the growth of vegetation, the accumulation of ice or debris or construction of bridges, buildings or levees within the flood channel.

The critical duration of intense rainfall might be only a few minutes for roof and parking lot drainage structures, while cumulative rainfall over several days would be critical for river basins. Extreme flood events often result from coincidence, such as unusually intense, warm rainfall melting a heavy snow pack, producing channel obstructions from floating ice and releasing small impoundments like beaver dams. Flood debris changing the drainage channel geometry is common when heavy flows move uprooted woody vegetation and flood-damaged structures and vehicles, including boats and railway equipment.

Ohio Flood History

Very extensive floods have been recorded in what is now known as the Ohio Valley as early as 1762. The flood of that year was recorded as being a very high torrent of water—it was about five feet higher than the flood of 1832, which for decades was remembered as one of the most disastrous. The 1832 event was the first great flood in which an accurate record was established. Starting on February 1, the ground of the countryside was covered with a deep blanket of snow, while pleasantly warm temperatures prevailed. For the next five days, the snow melted rapidly, and on February 6, the heavy rains began. On the eighth and ninth, it rained continuously, and by the tenth, the elevation of the Ohio River had started to attract the attention of the Cincinnati and Lawrenceburg communities. On the fourteenth, many merchants at Cincinnati began relocating their goods to the second stories of their homes and businesses as the river continued to rise rapidly until Saturday morning, February 18, when it came to a standstill.

The flood was of a most distressing character, and the Ohio River inflicted more damage when it overflowed its banks than what had been witnessed since the first settlement of the area. Nearly all the towns and communities along the Ohio River were inundated with floodwater in whole or in part. Fences and movable property were swept from all the bottomland farms on the river from Pittsburgh, Pennsylvania, to Louisville, Kentucky. Houses, barns, stored crops, grain and haystacks were seen floating down the river in great numbers. Hundreds of families in many communities instantly found themselves houseless.

In Hamilton County, a section of the banks of the Miami Canal caved in near Cincinnati, and there were other breaches of the canal elsewhere. Meanwhile, down at Cincinnati, the Ohio River hit forty feet above the low-water mark by late afternoon of February 11, and all buildings within two hundred yards of the river were flooded. The water covered between thirty to forty square blocks of the city, which was at that time mostly crowded near the river shore. By morning of the fourteenth, the eastern end of what is today known as Pete Rose Way in Cincinnati was under water. On Broadway, water stood twenty inches deep in the barrooms of two hotels as the river swelled to one mile in width.

The crest of the flood at Cincinnati did not come until the eighteenth of the month, when it hit sixty-four feet, three inches. There was great loss from all the flooding in Pennsylvania and West Virginia, as well as in Ohio. Wellsburg, West Virginia, was covered with water, and the people had to live temporarily in the upper stories of their homes. Warrenton, West Virginia, was demolished by this flood, while Marietta in Washington County, Ohio, was badly flooded, with water up to the eaves of a number of houses.

The flood reached its highest point on Feburary18, and two days later, the water had lowered only two feet, four inches. It was not until the twenty-fourth that the river finally returned to its banks. The entire bottom areas of Cincinnati and Lawrenceburg had been inundated with floodwater for about twelve days, which included six days while the flood was advancing and six days after the decline began. The March 3, 1832 edition of a local newspaper, the *Lawrenceburg Palladium*, published by David V. Culley, reported the following about the first recorded great flood to devastate the Ohio Valley:

> *February of 1832 was a wet month. Prior to the 10th of that month, there was a thaw in the weather with almost constant and sometimes heavy rains for a number of days. As a result, creeks, rivers and streams of all kinds rose to and above flood stage. The majority of bridges on the Cuyahoga River between the Portage County line and Cuyahoga Falls in Summit County were washed out. In fact, there were few bridges left along the Cuyahoga River in all of Cuyahoga County. Numerous mills were swept away as well, one of which was a five story building. When this mill went, nearly 2000 bushels of grain were lost. On the Black River at Elyria in Lorain County, another mill and its millstones were swept away, resulting in about a $12,000 loss there alone.*

In Stark County, mills and dams on the Nimishillen Creek suffered greatly, while all milldams on Newman's Creek were also destroyed. The Tuscarawas River was in flood as well, resulting in considerable damage to the Ohio-Erie Canal. Also, about twenty thousand board feet of lumber, which was to be used for a new bridge at Massillon, Stark County, was carried downstream by the floodwater.

Over in Trumbull County, a number of bridges were destroyed, including the one over the Mahoning River at Warren. In Franklin County, a stage trying to ford Alum Creek was swept into the raging waters, with the loss of two horses and the mail.

At Steubenville in Jefferson County, the Ohio River was in high flood stage by February 11, 1832, as it then was close to five feet higher than any previously known flood. Many people living near the river survived with only the clothes on their backs. Water Street was just that, as it was under eight feet of water. Houses were lifted off their foundations by the floodwater, and the river was full of lumber, haystacks, grain and various buildings, all of which were floating along on the water.

During the years 1847, 1866 and 1875, the Ohio Valley experienced more floods. Although these floods were noteworthy, they resulted in far less damage than the disastrous floods of the consecutive years of 1883 and 1884. In February 1883, the Ohio River surpassed its crest of 1832 at Cincinnati, reaching sixty-six feet, four inches. Exactly one year later, floodwater struck again in the Ohio Valley, reaching seventy-one feet, one inch at Cincinnati, a record high that was to stand until 1937. Toward the end of January 1884, Ohio was experiencing milder temperatures than usual, causing rapid melting of the midwinter snow that covered the state. This, of course, brought the water of many of the streams to the tops of their banks. As February began, these streams began to go beyond their banks into a flooding condition. Adding to the melting snow cover, the warm temperatures fueled heavy rains that increased the rising waters. By the afternoon of February 7, the Ohio River at Cincinnati, Ohio, had reached a height of sixty-one feet, one inch. As the rains continued the fall, the gasworks in Cincinnati was inundated with floodwater, and the streets were in darkness. The local relief committee appropriated $10,000 for immediate aid to help more than twelve thousand families who were made homeless. Two oil tanks broke open during the evening of the sixth, and this sent an oil slick floating out on the floodwater. Most of the streetcar lines had been abandoned by the seventh, and the main part of Cincinnati was virtually cut off from any communication with the suburbs, including by telegraph.

Appeals went out to Lake Erie communities such as Cleveland, Toledo and Sandusky for boats.

Just across the state line in Indiana, all business at Lawrenceburg came to a complete halt, and the citizens of that town were anxiously fleeing the rising floodwater. Like the surrounding Cincinnati communities, there was no communication by railroad, telephone or telegraph with Lawrenceburg. On February 6, farther up the Ohio River at Pittsburgh, Pennsylvania, the Ohio reached its highest stage since 1852. According to the *Holmes County Farmer*, "Miles of property on the south side of the City of Pittsburg and in Allegheny City are submerged. All the mills and factories on both rivers have suspended. Hundreds of families have vacated their homes. Cellars and first floors in the lower business section are under water. Railway travel is greatly retarded and on some roads suspended." Every street from Pennsylvania Avenue to Sharpsburg (a five-mile stretch) was under between one and ten feet of water.

Back in Ohio, the Scioto River at Chillicothe in Ross County washed away several bridges and a frame house, and one person was listed as having drowned. At Louisville, Kentucky, the Ohio reached within three feet of the previous year's mark and was still rising. The towns of Jeffersonville and New Albany, Indiana, were almost totally under water, while the village of Shepherdsville on the Salt River was washed away. By February 8, 1884, the Ohio River at Pittsburgh had begun to descend after having flooded out well over 5,750 businesses and about 29,400 homes. The ruined economy placed more than 44,500 people out of work, and there were heavy damages and a significant loss of timber at the headwaters of the Allegheny River. While the Ohio River at Pittsburgh was falling on February 8, the Muskingum and Tuscarawas Rivers in Coshocton County, Ohio were still on the rise. The entire west end of the town of Coshocton was under water, and the countryside for miles around was covered by the floodwater. Railroad trains on the Panhandle Line had discontinued service, and there was considerable damage to the tracks at Ironton in Lawrence County and Mingo in Jefferson County. In addition, more than one mile of track was reported to have been washed out elsewhere in the state. In some places, the banks of the Ohio Canal were also badly damaged.

Near the Ohio state line at Wheeling, West Virginia, the fairgrounds were said to have been in a state of complete ruin. Three houses had come floating down to Wheeling from upriver on the seventh. On that date, "houses, barns, bridges, straw and haystacks" were seen floating past Wheeling the entire day. There were fifteen thousand people homeless at Wheeling, with

Throughout the Midwest, rail transportation was stopped for months because rail line tracks were uprooted for miles, as seen in this photo taken in Tuscarawas County, Ohio. *CML.*

ten thousand having absolutely no provisions for their welfare. At Wellsville, located in Columbiana County, Ohio, the community suffered heavily from the floodwater. Heavy rains fell all day and night on February 6, and when combined with the melting snow and ice, they swelled the rivers and streams to enormous sizes. The Ohio River reached the highest stage ever witnessed, and a large sawmill that supposedly came from Industry, Pennsylvania, floated by intact and still filled with lumber. Also, at Wellsville, Ohio, the gas went off, and water was flowing five to ten feet deep through town from one end to the other. In some places, the water rose above the second stories of houses, and in one area of the town, the water was fifteen to twenty feet deep. The rooftops of houses could barely be seen.

The floodwater at Smith's Ferry, Pennsylvania, stood two feet above the high-water mark of 1832, and the community was completely under water. Refineries were also under water, and hundreds of barrels of oil were swept away. The Columbiana County bridge over the Little Beaver Creek became dislodged and was floating on the water. In Steubenville, located in Jefferson County, Ohio, by the Ohio River, the entire lower portion of the city was under water, and eleven thousand kegs of nails were submerged at the Jefferson Iron Works. The potteries at East Liverpool in Columbiana County, Ohio, were flooded, and all communication with that city was cut off except for one telegraph wire to Cleveland.

By February 8, one-fourth of Zanesville in Muskingum County, Ohio, was flooded. A railroad embankment had been holding back the water there, but when the water came rushing over that at 2:00 a.m. on the eighth, half of the second ward was flooded within five minutes. People had to scramble to the second floors of their homes so they could be rescued by boat.

Returning to Cincinnati in Hamilton County, Ohio, rain began falling steadily at 4:00 a.m. on the tenth, and the Ohio River there was still steadily rising. It surpassed the 1832 flood crest and had risen to 65 feet, 5.25 inches by the eleventh. Meanwhile, on February 10 at Wheeling, West Virginia, some fifty houses became jammed against one another on the south end of that town. About four tons of mail, the first mail in four days, arrived at Wheeling, West Virginia, on the tenth. Bedclothes there were in short supply, as all blankets in the city had been distributed to those in need. Wagons full of supplies had been coming in all day on the tenth from places as far as twenty miles away on the Ohio side of the river. In the stretch from Wellsburg to Moundsville, West Virginia, an estimated twenty thousand people needed to be fed and clothed.

On the Ohio side of the Ohio River, an engineer on the Scioto Valley Railway waded out of Portsmouth in Scioto County and then walked twenty-four miles north to Piketon in Pike County. There he sent a telegraph message stating that the water at Portsmouth was five feet higher than in the flood of the previous year. One steamship had floated aground and was lying in the water on a sidewalk. People were entering and exiting a hotel at Portsmouth through the second-story windows, and three houses in the city were on fire.

Rain fell heavily along all of the Ohio River counties during the afternoon and evening of February 10. At Gallipolis in Gallia County, the river was rising at the rate of three-fourths of an inch per hour and was seven feet higher than in 1883. In Ripley, Ohio, in Brown County, the floodwater had swept some houses away, and a large amount of tobacco hanging in barns in lower sections had sustained great damage. The evening of the tenth found the Ohio River at Ripley five inches higher than it had been twenty-four hours earlier.

Rain was still falling heavily at Cincinnati on the morning of the eleventh. Boating at Lawrenceburg, Indiana, was becoming dangerous due to the swift current, and more houses were being taken from their foundations. Upriver a little way at New Richmond in Clermont County, Ohio, water was in every building, and the town had no communication with outside areas except by skiff. One-third of the people in that town depended on outside help, and while hundreds of homes were filled with water, some thirty-five houses

The residents of Lawrenceburg, Indiana, located down the Ohio River from Cincinnati, worked desperately to reinforce this levee break with sandbags. *LOC.*

had floated completely off their foundations. Meanwhile, across the river in Kentucky, the village of Rural had been washed off the map, with only two of the thirty-six houses there remaining.

Farther upriver at Pomeroy in Meigs County, Ohio, there were five thousand people camped on the hills and described as in terrible want for food and shelter since more than 150 homes had floated away. Boats were landing at the steps of the courthouse, and practically every businessman in the city was bankrupt due to the flood. Of course, the coal mines at Syracuse in Meigs County were flooded, and at Middleport, also in Meigs County, a house (with a woman sitting on the gable end of it) went floating by during the morning of the eleventh.

On February 12 in Cincinnati at 12:30 a.m., the Ohio River continued rising at the rate of one inch per hour. By 4:00 a.m., the river there was up to sixty-seven feet, seven inches. On Steamboat Square, the second stories of buildings were flooded, and all trains with the exception of the Cincinnati Northern had to stay outside the city. Across the river, nearly half of Newport, Kentucky, was under water, and fifteen thousand people there were without shelter.

In Pomeroy, Ohio, on the thirteenth, the situation began to get worse. Water was eleven feet deep on Second Street, and only the tall industrial chimneys of factories were visible. That same day, all of Portsmouth, Ohio, was under floodwater, with three-fourths of the city under water rooftop deep. Half the people there lost all they had, and 120 homes were carried away by the river. More than 500 other houses had been destroyed. No mail had come there for five days. Strong winds and heavy rains hit Cincinnati during the nights of February 12 and 13. A short way downriver, Lawrenceburg, Indiana, was running out of coal and coal oil. A total of 50 homes there had been swept away, and four hundred pianos and organs were floating in the water. That city was completely cut off from the outside world.

By now, the majority of Aurora, Indiana was under water, while Jeffersonville, Indiana, was entirely submerged. Point Pleasant, West Virginia, was totally submerged under six feet of water. Half of Buffalo, West Virginia, was under water, and the Kanawha River was three to five miles wide well above its junction with the Ohio River. All along the Ohio River from Wheeling, West Virginia, to Cairo, Illinois, a multitude of villages and small communities had either been completely destroyed or at least had very little intact.

Rain fell continuously on the thirteenth and during that night until 2:00 a.m. on the fourteenth. At Newport, Kentucky, twenty more houses were lost to the river during that night, and more were on the verge of being swallowed up. The climax of the flood at Cincinnati came at 1:00 p.m. on the fourteenth, when the Ohio River reached a height of seventy-one feet, one inch.

On the sixteenth, the federal relief boat *Stockdale* docked at Marietta, Ohio, with $50,000 of supplies on board. Sixty homes at Marietta had been washed away. On the other side of the river, every railroad bridge in Wood County, West Virginia, had been swept away by floodwater, and Parkersburg had lost eighty houses.

Twentieth-Century Flooding Puts on a Different Face

Having endured these nineteenth-century flood events, many communities felt that they were flood savvy and had a good understanding of what to do when a flood occurred. With a new century approaching, this false confidence proved detrimental in many cases.

The 1913 flood was America's most widespread flood to that date. Once the freezing rains started and the flooding began, it continued for days across the Midwest and to the East Coast. Some people drowned in their attics and others on the roads when they tried to flee. It killed more than seven hundred people and left millions devastated and homeless following the destruction of hundreds of thousands of homes and buildings. In truth, the full scope of destruction extended far beyond the Ohio Valley states (which include Ohio, Indiana, Illinois, Pennsylvania, Kentucky and West Virginia). Fourteen states in all, including Michigan, New York, New Jersey, Vermont, Tennessee, Arkansas, Louisiana and Nebraska, and every major and minor river east of the Mississippi were also affected.

The calamity of the Great Flood of 1913 began on Easter Sunday, March 23, with a massive tornado-producing storm that tore its way through the state of Nebraska. A series of eight distinct tornados killed 150 people and injured 400 in the thriving city of Omaha, Nebraska. The storm's path extended forty miles and was estimated to have been about one-quarter to a half mile wide.

Easter Sunday in Omaha began under a cloudy sky, with rain threatening but never falling on the city, and by noon, the skies had brightened to the point where the sun was beginning to peek through. In the afternoon, the skies darkened again as a massive storm system moved into the area from western Nebraska. On Sunday morning, the storm system brought snow to the Colorado Rockies and high winds to Denver. The first tornado from the storm touched down at 5:20 p.m. just outside Craig, Nebraska. It continued into Iowa without causing major damage. A second tornado touched down ten minutes later at about 5:30 p.m. near Ithaca and claimed the first casualties of the day as it traveled on through Yutan. Another two rural tornados followed.

At 5:45 p.m. a tornado touched down near Kramer. This tornado raced northeast and reached the outskirts of Omaha at about 6:00 p.m. The Omaha tornado followed the path of Little Papillion Creek as it entered the city. It moved through the west side of the community parallel to the Missouri Pacific Railroad, destroying several small workers' cottages in the area. The force of the tornado was so massive that steel railroad cars were subsequently found pierced by pieces of shattered lumber from the demolished homes. By the time the tornado reached Dewey Avenue, it was five blocks wide. When it reached Farnam Hill, the twister followed a shallow valley through the upscale neighborhood. The large mansions of Farnam were no match for the winds, and many houses were torn to pieces, along with a number of prestigious landmarks of the Gold Coast Historic District, including the Joslyn Castle, which sustained considerable damage. Some buildings—such as the Duchesne Academy, which was nearly totally destroyed—were discovered torn in half, with pipes and supports dangling in the air.

During an Easter program at North Twenty-fourth and Lake Streets in the Near North Side neighborhood, a sizable gathering of African American citizens were enjoying a splendid Sunday performance when the tornado obliterated the building they were in and killed well over two dozen people. Many masonry buildings in this small commercial district took similar hits, and it was in this area of the city that the majority of the fatalities occurred.

A streetcar running down North Twenty-fourth Street in north Omaha encountered the tornado near this area. It was only due to the quick actions of operator Ord Hensley that every passenger on the streetcar survived. Afterward, several newspaper photographers took pictures of the wreckage, eventually dubbing it the "Streetcar of Death" because no one remaining on board the tram could have survived given the scope of damage.

The F4 tornado skirted the downtown area and moved over the Missouri River into Council Bluffs, Iowa. By this time, the winds were starting to

The aftermath of the Easter Sunday Omaha, Nebraska tornado. This was one of three severe weather fronts that collided over Indiana and Ohio, causing the torrential rains that led to flooding. *LOC.*

The Easter Sunday 1913 Omaha tornado left this business district looking like a barren wasteland. The storm front continued moving east, causing great havoc. *LOC.*

die down, and while Council Bluffs sustained some damage, it escaped the devastation the tornado had inflicted on Omaha.

Unfortunately, the only warning anyone had was the sharp and rapid fall of barometric pressure and air temperature. Very few people had time to seek shelter. Of the 150 people who died, 103 of the casualties occurred in Omaha, and in the aftermath of the tornado, a cold front moved into Omaha and caused further misery, as newly homeless residents struggled to escape the cold, snowy weather. The same storm system that struck Nebraska also created a huge dust storm in Topeka, Kansas. On Sunday night, it spawned another deadly tornado that hit Terre Haute, Indiana, and claimed another fifty lives. On Monday and Tuesday, the storm ushered heavy torrential rains and wind into the Midwest, and this set the stage for extensive regional flooding.

Enter the Grand Champion of Ohio Floods

In 1897, 1898 and 1907, there were serious floods in Ohio, but the greatest of all time for the state as a whole was the Great Flood of 1913. Every major river valley, except the Ohio, experienced record high water, and more than one hundred cities and towns were inundated. Heavy and prolonged rainfall on frozen or saturated ground was the principal cause. Between March 21 and 27, about 24 million cubic yards of water poured down on Ohio, enough to have raised Lake Erie, with an area of ten thousand square miles, approximately four feet. This rain fell on land that had long been deforested, whose swamps had been drained and whose flood plains had been converted to building sites, thus producing conditions that enabled even more serious flooding. In five days, beginning on Easter Sunday, March 23, Ohio received an average of six inches of rain on already saturated ground. The Great Miami and Sandusky watersheds each had nine inches, the Cuyahoga and Mahoning each received eight and the Muskingum and Scioto each had seven inches of waterfall.

The heaviest deluge of precipitation occurred at the headwaters of the streams, causing floods from their sources to their mouths. The source, or headwaters, of a river or stream is the farthest place in that river or stream from its estuary or confluence (meeting) with another body of water, as measured along the course of the river. All over the state of Ohio, record high water was reported, as detailed in the following chart:

LOCATION	RIVER	CRITICAL MARK	1913 HIGH	BEYOND PREVIOUS RECORD
Zanesville	Muskingum	25.0 ft.	51.8 ft.	15.0 ft.
Chillicothe	Scioto	14.5 ft.	37.8 ft.	9.5 ft.
Dayton	Great Miami	18.0 ft.	29.3 ft.	8.0 ft.
Defiance	Maumee	10.0 ft.	28.0 ft.	12.0 ft.
Fremont	Sandusky	10.0 ft.	21.5 ft.	5.0 ft.
Youngstown	Mahoning	5.0 ft.	22.9 ft.	7.1 ft.

The speed at which the waters traveled during this flood compounded their destructive force. At Chillicothe, at its crest, the Scioto River was flowing at a rate of 260,000 cubic feet of water per second. That is roughly ten times the normal discharge. The volume figures for Dayton were about the same. But at Hamilton, Ohio, the discharge, which is typically around 25,000 feet per second for a channel capacity of 100,000, reached the astounding level of 352,000 feet per second.

The calamity and misery was universal in Ohio. More than twenty thousand homes were completely destroyed, and nearly thirty-six thousand more were rendered uninhabitable. The Miami Valley alone suffered property damage estimated in 1913 at $100 million, of which the destruction in Dayton accounted for about half of the flood's damage in that region. The property loss in the Scioto and Sandusky Valleys totaled about $40 million, with Columbus suffering $15 million in damage. The total property damage amounted to about $180 million, but the full cost of the flood probably reached closer to $250 million (or $5.6 billion in today's dollars). Well over 500 known deaths were directly caused by the flood, and hundreds of missing persons were never found. Columbus and Dayton each reported about 100 fatalities, but that number is in doubt and still considered very low by many today. Hamilton suffered 159 deaths, and Piqua reported at least 50 in the wake of the flood. During the weeks after the flood, many victims died from exposure and the mental stress they had endured. In many cases, general health and well-being were permanently broken or mental breakdowns resulted. At least 32 people had to be committed to the Dayton hospital for the mentally insane, with diagnostic summaries charging their disability to their flood experiences.

In Zanesville, about one-fourth of the city was inundated, and unfortunately, the area affected was the most heavily populated section of town. Some 600

Floodwater from the Muskingum River pushed railroad cars off the tracks in Zanesville, Ohio. *CML.*

buildings were reported to have been swept away, the Putnam area was laid in ruins and Muskingum and Linden Avenues were no more. In Columbus, the four main bridges connecting the east and west sides and a number of railroad bridges were completely destroyed. The homeless there, including residents of 345 houses totally wrecked, numbered ten thousand, and 3,400 businesses were forced to close for an average of two weeks. Chillicothe had an average of four thousand homeless, which accounted for more than one-fourth of the community's population. Tiffin and Fremont, Ohio, had nearly 70 buildings and houses carried away or destroyed and 1,000 homes flooded and damaged. Half of Massillon, Ohio, was under water, and three thousand were homeless. Youngstown and Cleveland industrial and manufacturing plants were affected so severely that well over seventy-five thousand people were put out of work. Piqua lost more than 200 homes, and in Troy, where 50 percent of the town was underwater, some 50 houses were washed downriver.

Hamilton was a city of total desolation, with nearly 50 percent of it lying under water that was as much as eight feet deep; 200 homes were carried away, and many other homes and buildings were destroyed by the water and by fires, which added to the chaos. One entire street was washed away for several blocks, and on the streets, the current scoured ravines fifteen to twenty-five feet deep. In Marietta, 33 percent of the community was

The flood currents sent the entire inventory of this lumberyard floating through the community into homes and businesses. *LOC.*

Two train locomotives derailed after floodwater washed the railroad tie timbers away and eroded the bed. *CML.*

inundated, with the Muskingum River reaching a record high of sixty feet. About 67 percent of the houses and the entire business section were flooded; 115 houses were destroyed, and the two bridges across the Muskingum were wiped out. About 80 percent of Ironton, Ohio, was under water, rendering 8,000 of the 13,500 residents completely homeless. Also, approximately 80 percent of Portsmouth was under water, and nearly half of the people were driven from their homes by floodwater and fires. About 1,000 people in Ripley were homeless, leaving only 800 with their residences unaffected by the flood. Cincinnati's floodwater reached nearly seventy feet, and the outbreak of fires only compounded the misery in the Queen City.

The industrial town of Dayton was the hardest-hit spot nationwide. There, 2,000 homes were washed away or completely demolished by the flood, 4,500 were seriously damaged and 15,000 required major rehabilitation. A number of serious fires (due to broken gas lines) added to the horror. More than eighty-five thousand people were standing in breadlines for two weeks. Some of their losses included 15,350 pianos, 25,800 clocks, 528 automobiles, 2,934 cash registers and every plate glass window in the downtown business section. After the water had subsided, the community was covered by an awful stench from the bodies of more than two thousand horses and other domestic animals that were found dead on the streets.

Throughout the Ohio Valley, most of the communities had water and gas utilities, electrical, telegraph, and sewerage facilities completely out of service, and bridges and transportation lines were destroyed or badly damaged. Two Pennsylvania Railroad trains fell into Ohio floodwater when bridges gave way, and on the railroad track line, twenty-four bridges were destroyed and fifty damaged, with the majority of them in Ohio. Everywhere the flood traveled, it left a sea of yellow or brown mud and ugly heaps of brush, wreckage, refuse and filth. Buildings were smeared inside and out with mud, and they retained an offensive odor for months after the flood. The magnificent record of help, caring and assistance given to the flood victims, and of the rehabilitation and restoration of commerce in the damaged areas, will forever be a story of great merit never fully told.

West Columbus Caught by Surprise

It is interesting that in the Ohio capital city of Columbus, the 1913 flood inflicted the majority of its devastation in the area initially settled by the city's early pioneer community. The area known as Franklinton is located adjacent to the confluence of the Scioto and Olentangy Rivers. For most of the nineteenth century and during the early days of Franklinton, the area had been the site of a dozen major floods dating to back 1798. However, none of these earlier flood events was as devastating as the great surge of water that swept through the Columbus waterfront March 23–27, 1913. The main causes of the flood were extremely heavy torrential rains, melting snow and significant water runoff over ground that was already saturated to its limit.

The Franklinton community was particularly vulnerable because it was perilously situated in the Scioto River's western flood plain. The deluge of water, ranging in depth from three to twenty-two feet, inundated nearly 4,850 homes and businesses and killed ninety-six people while forcing an additional twenty thousand to flee west to the high ground of the Hilltop area. As mentioned, the flood started when the frozen ground of winter refused to yield to an overnight transition to warm spring temperatures and nearly a week of constant wind and rain. While many in Columbus got wet and had to swim for their lives, strangely enough, those who stayed dry on high ground found themselves abandoning homes and businesses and running in total fear of being engulfed by high water. This disaster gave rise to a sense of civic determination to control future flooding that, of course, by its simple nature, cannot be stopped.

On Easter morning, March 23, 1913, as the west Columbus residents began gathering in their churches and chapels to celebrate the grace of God, many found comfort that the warm weather of spring appeared to be unfolding. Since the day before had been unseasonably warm, many people were anticipating an equally pleasant Easter Sunday. No one was ready for the misery and devastation that was about to commence as a result of several massive storm fronts colliding over the Midwest. For all who lived in Franklinton, their lives would never be the same. Many of them lost their homes, possessions, livelihoods and even loved ones so dear to them. Life on the west side of Columbus would undergo the greatest disaster of its history, and the people who narrowly survived the flood would carry the haunting memories of their experience for the rest of their lives.

Instead of a joyful, sunny Easter morning, the uplifted spirits of many people were quickly dampened by a cold, heavy, torrential rainstorm. The storm that started at dawn on Easter Sunday persisted throughout the day and was intensified occasionally by heavy rain and extremely strong gusts of wind. By the time church was dismissed, all thoughts of a pleasantly peaceful and mild spring day had totally disappeared.

The rain began tapering off at midnight but resumed at full force again early Monday morning with a continuous downpour that continued well into Tuesday. On Monday, March 24, the local *Columbus Evening Dispatch* newspaper reported that although the rain would continue, the community had no reason to fear the storms that wrecked property and destroyed life in Nebraska and the upper Missouri Valley region on Easter Sunday. The local weather service office stated that the storm was over the Great Lakes and moving east rapidly. The severe weather storm would miss Columbus, but the rain would continue in the vicinity through Tuesday, with temperatures dropping. Consequently, people went about their business and children went to school as if Tuesday would be just another mild, rainy day. The Monday and Tuesday rains brought a total of six inches, with three inches falling during the last twelve hours of the storm on Tuesday. The Easter Sunday downpour of rain dumped an additional three inches of storm water on central Ohio.

The people living in the Franklinton community arose Tuesday morning and generally went about their day as usual. By 9:00 a.m., the Scioto River was just about to compromise its banks, as the currents lapped ominously at the top of the earthen flood levee. Soon, the levee began to spill muddy-brown water and floating debris over its edge. Flooding in Franklinton was no longer a possibility but rather a front-door reality for the people living in

The south bank levee of the Scioto River failed and sent a tsunami-like torrent of floodwater into the west Columbus area of Franklinton. *CML.*

the low-lying areas of this historic west Columbus community. The residents of Franklinton had experienced flooding previously, as recently as 1907 and 1898, so they were not unfamiliar with flooding in their area. From its earliest settlement in 1797 until that time, the community had experienced a total of thirteen floods, with several being rather significant. But these previous events were marginal at best when compared to the calamity and devastation that was about to take place.

Most Columbus residents then still recalled the floodwater that occurred in the spring of 1898. But that floodwater entered the Franklinton community very gradually. The floodwater started by quietly filling basements, and then it slowly began seeping into the ground floors of homes, factories and businesses. The flood of 1898 was by no means a killer like the one that was about to wreak havoc on Franklinton, but it had done its share of damage by shutting down the city transportation system, businesses and schools and essentially paralyzing the community for a number of days. This time, a solid wall of water, like a huge inland tsunami, was about to engulf Franklinton. And like a tsunami, it would strike with surprisingly swift and tremendous power. The speed and suddenness of this assault caught everyone off guard.

The horrifying character of this flood was, oddly enough, defined by natural events. It developed out of a simultaneous collision of three colossal air masses. One was a stream of moisture-laden tropical air that started in the Gulf of Mexico and then headed northward toward the Midwest. As it proceeded north, it initiated very brief early summer–like weather wherever it went. As this storm front continued, it traveled through Georgia and Tennessee. It then entered the Ohio Valley through Kentucky and headed straight for Cincinnati, Ohio.

The second mass of air was an icy blast of frigid Canadian air that had formed near the mouth of the St. Lawrence River. As it accelerated southwestward from Quebec to Toronto, through Detroit, Michigan, and on into Toledo, its strength and fury escalated to a gale-force wind.

The third air mass was an eruption nearly matching a hurricane in its proportions that formed ominously in the Great Plains of central Nebraska. It was this weather that had devastated the city of Omaha on Easter Sunday with a series of tornados that injured hundreds and left thousands homeless. It pounded Des Moines, Iowa, and then raged across the state of Illinois. As it approached Indianapolis and increased in destructive power, it prepared to meet the air masses coming in from the north and south.

These three powerful air masses, each spinning forward like a railroad locomotive out of control, finally collided into one another other in a battle of wills. The battlefield was a 3,500-square-mile area that stretched from Indianapolis in the west to Fort Wayne and Lima in the north; Hamilton, Ohio, in the south; and Zanesville in the east. The countryside beneath this severe and deadly weather was already at its saturation limit. The land had been soaked by extensive runoff from the snow and ice accumulated during the long and hard winter that resulted following the eruption of the Novarupta Volcano in Alaska the previous year. The severe winter was a result of the cooling effect on the atmosphere caused by a volcanic winter that followed the eruption. A number of early spring rains exacerbated the situation to the point that toward the end of March, the land could no longer absorb any water.

For many, it is almost impossible to comprehend the unprecedented, massive quantity of precipitation created by the collision of these three tremendously powerful air masses. As they clashed and the heavens parted, thick blankets of heavy rainfall deposited on average of nine inches of precipitation on every foot of the 3,500 square miles of countryside below these storms.

What resulted afterward would have been incomprehensible to most people before the flood. Nearly 4 trillion gallons of water were deposited on a land area whose surface was already saturated to its full limit. To understand this massive amount of water, consider that 1.6 million gallons of water flows over Niagara Falls every second. At this rate, the volume of water flowing over Niagara Falls would take about four weeks to equal the amount of rain that fell during the Easter flood of 1913. It was as much water as it would take to fill a canyon that measured 6.25 miles in length by 100 feet deep by 1.00 mile in width.

Just before 11:00 a.m. on Tuesday morning, people living near the levee at the foot of Broad Street heard a peculiar roaring sound. The noise turned out to be the south bank levee that, after being weakened by the pressure of millions of gallons of violently rushing water, suddenly failed and gave way. A huge wall of water that resembled a small tsunami picked up speed as it gathered force after breaking through the levee and fanned out rapidly over the low-lying areas of Franklinton. And like a tsunami, in a matter of minutes, the area from the Scioto River to the Hilltop area was submerged under between eight and twenty-two feet of floodwater. The Columbus Franklinton neighborhood is bordered by the Scioto River on the north and east, Harmon Avenue on the east, Stimmel Road on the south and Schultz Avenue on the west. West Broad Street is Franklinton's main east–west throughway. Franklinton is the neighborhood immediately west of downtown, and much of the land lies below the water level of the Scioto and Olentangy Rivers; a flood wall is required to contain the rivers and protect the area from devastating floods. One of the main reasons Franklinton was one of the first settlements in the area was because the fertile, low-lying bottomland was ideal for farming, and the Scioto River served as a direct connection to the Ohio River and beyond.

One of the flood survivors shared her terrifying experience, which began with her father, who was employed by the city. He worked in an office located on the upper floor of the new high-rise Wyandot Building on Broad Street, just two blocks from the Scioto River. From this vantage point, he had a panoramic view of the riverfront area. As the morning advanced, he became increasingly alarmed as he observed the danger mounting with the rising of the river. At 10:30 a.m., because of his concern for his family, he telephoned his home on the west side and specifically warned his wife to gather up their children and head immediately for the high ground in the hilltop area. Upon hanging up the phone, he ran immediately from his office and headed toward the city horse stables located on McKinley Avenue. He felt that his first priority was to release the city's horses so they would be given a fighting chance to survive what was to come rather than sentence them to certain drowning while being abandoned and tied to their stalls.

A bird's-eye view of downtown Columbus during the high water of the 1913 flood. All of the main bridges were washed away except for the Rich Street Bridge, which the city had previously condemned and scheduled for demolition. *CML.*

The floodwater of the Scioto River encroaching on the state penitentiary on Goodale Avenue. *CML.*

At the time of his phone call, his wife had been cooking lunch. She turned off the stove, where she had a pot of beans that had been simmering, and assembled the children with a determined shout. In a pen located in the backyard, there were two pet rabbits that had been awarded blue ribbons at the Ohio State Fair. She was not about to leave them behind. Her youngest daughter (the flood survivor sharing the story) was told to gather the rabbits as her mother went about locking the house.

Just before the levee collapsed, local police were racing up and down streets, shouting warnings to the residents living in the low-lying districts. Finally, the order was given to evacuate all homes immediately, without stopping to pack any belongings. All streetcar traffic was abandoned.

Once the family reached the street and could see the bizarre panic unfolding around them, the mother became distraught. Her first concern was that without transportation, how was she going to escape to safety with her children and pet rabbits? Although frantic, she was a determined mother. She began to quickly walk the family down the street. She noticed that the young man who worked at the neighborhood grocery was galloping in his horse-pulled delivery wagon to their home. Apparently, the young man had romantic feelings for one of the daughters and was bringing the wagon to rescue the family. The entire family quickly piled into the wagon, and the young man urged the nervous horse to run at top speed as floodwater rushed into the street and soon flowed past the hubcaps of the wagon. Although this family narrowly escaped, about ninety-six other people perished in Columbus due to the cold floodwater.

One eyewitness to the deaths of many flood victims from the swirling waters near Calvary Cemetery was Charles Clinger. He was a gardener who resided on Calvary Avenue near Mound Street. Throughout the night on Tuesday, he heard people screaming for help in their uprooted homes drifting on the raging water past his residence. Clinger's home was located on high ground just south of the Calvary cemetery. When he saw the water rising early on Tuesday, Clinger ran through the West Mound Street area warning people to leave their homes and seek refuge on higher ground. Some people laughed at him, and others scoffed at the idea of danger. Once the levee broke, those same people suddenly became victims with nowhere to go. Clinger and his family saw houses torn like cardboard boxes from their foundations and sent floating downstream.

One example of how suddenly the water rushed into the area is how a streetcar en route to safety was overtaken by the wall of water and was washed a quarter of a mile off its track. Unfortunately, the conductor and his six passengers were trapped inside the streetcar and immediately drowned.

This was one of several streetcars in Columbus that was caught in the torrent of floodwater after the Franklinton levee broke. In one case, the tram conductor and all passengers perished. *CML.*

Another flood survivor told of his flood experience as a small boy. He was six years old at the time of the flood, and his family resided in Franklinton. He recalled that his father took hold of his hand in a bone-crushing grip and dragged him down the street as they were running for their lives. As they approached the nearest streetcar station, the young boy saw manhole covers being tossed several feet into the air by geysers created by the great pressure of the water surging through the underground sewer pipes. "When I saw that, I was never more scared in my life," he confided. The boy and his father jumped aboard a streetcar speeding away from the low areas. The car, overloaded with desperate folks like themselves, finally reached the Town Street Bridge, only to be stopped from crossing by a policeman who had blocked traffic from the bridge. "It ain't safe to go across," he barked. "That bridge will give way any minute."

Somehow, the sight of those terrified faces of the passengers must have moved the policeman to reconsider because in the next moment, he moved the barricade and yelled to the driver, "OK—gun it!" The driver shifted the gears, and under full acceleration, the streetcar barreled across the bridge. Just as they touched the east bank of the Scioto River, the bridge collapsed into the swirling floodwater. "We were the last streetcar over the Town Street Bridge," the survivor commented sadly, "and I'll never forget it!"

As the Scioto continued to crest, the Sandusky Street levee also lost its ability to contain the unruly river. The levee went down in the midst of a large deluge that washed out a railroad embankment and quickly flooded the low districts between the river and Sandusky Street. Mrs. Emil Wallace, a resident of the lowlands in the southwest part of the city, ran toward a hill when she spied the onrushing water. By running as fast as she could, Mrs. Wallace had barely reached safety when a vicious wave of muddy river water smacked her with such a force that it knocked her off her feet. Within seconds, the ice-cold water was up to her chin. Although Mrs. Wallace survived the flood, the home she left behind was overtaken and completely submerged.

Hundreds of working folks—including fathers, sons, brothers, sisters, daughters and even grandparents—had gone to work on the east side of the river that morning. By that afternoon, they were completely cut off from their homes and families on the west side of the river. With little or no means of communication available, including courier, they had no way of determining whether or not their loved ones had survived the disaster. Many of these people congregated in large groups on the east edge of the river. There they kept an agonizing vigil, watching the relentless progress of the flood, morning and night, for several days.

By late Monday, practically all of Franklinton was under water or washed away by the strong currents. It was soon apparent to many that taking refuge in the second floor of the mostly wood-frame houses was not a guarantee of safety. House after house was lifted off its foundation, spun around by the strength of the current and washed down the river, with frightened people clinging precariously to the roof. People along the shore could only watch helplessly as houses containing men, women and children floated past them, collapsed and dissolved into the water. In a scene of horror, there were numerous bodies of dead people, horses, cows and other domestic animals floating in a grim procession past the onlookers.

After the floodwater receded, there were many heartfelt stories of personal heroism that were related and shared. Charles W. Underwood had been working as a carpenter in Columbus before the floodwater inflicted great sorrow on his life and family. Starting in the afternoon of Tuesday, March 25, at 2:00 p.m. and lasting until nightfall of the following day, Underwood firmly held two babies in his arms while he also clutched tenuously to the branches of a tree adjacent to the west end of Green Lawn Cemetery. He and the two infants had been caught by the force of the floodwater current and tossed about for practically a mile

The break in the levee that flooded the Franklinton community in west Columbus. This photo was taken the following week after the floodwater had subsided and shows the thirty-six-inch cast-iron water main that was unearthed. *CML.*

Looking north from Broad Street along the bank of the Scioto River. Many of these buildings were originally built in this lowland area during the era of canal commerce. *CML.*

This surviving horse was temporarily stuck in flood debris in Columbus. Unfortunately, domestic work animals accounted for most of the flood deaths. *CML.*

before he was able to secure himself to a tree. One baby belonged to a neighbor, and the other was his own child. As he firmly held both infants in his arms, Underwood had to watch, powerlessly, as his older twelve-year-old daughter, grasping another limb of the same tree, weakened from exposure to the cold and died. Her fragile body swayed limply as it hung over the branch. A woman who had also taken refuge in the same tree weakened and lost her grip within close reach of Underwood. Since holding the infants afforded him no free hand to offer her, she slipped quietly into the churning, ice-cold floodwater. As night nearly set on Wednesday evening, a relief boat finally arrived to save him and the two infants in his care.

The dangerous task of rescuing the flood victims was started by mobilizing and acquiring resources in a unique manner. Opha Moore appropriately noted in *History of Franklin County, Ohio*, written in 1930, that one of the most outstanding heroic figures—who stood so significantly and clearly apart that no open-minded and impartial historian would overlook him—was Robert F. Wolfe, the owner and publisher of the *Columbus Dispatch* newspaper at the time of the flood. On the morning of March 25, Columbus mayor George J. Karb asked Wolfe to help in spearheading vital rescue operations of flood victims in the Franklinton area of Columbus. The one resource that was in

This family is being rescued by rowboat and transported to a relief center. Many boats were brought to Columbus from Buckeye Lake by rail to be used as rescue craft. *CML.*

extremely short supply was boats. So Wolfe headed up a team of *Dispatch* employees to help bring boats from Buckeye Lake, some forty miles east of Columbus in Licking County. The *Dispatch* chartered a special cargo transport train on the Ohio Electric railway line to shuttle the boats. The train was made up of a passenger car and two flatcars. Some gas-powered boats that had been outfitted for duck hunting were located on Buckeye Lake. As those craft were being made ready, locks were smashed on boathouses to get to as many stored boats as possible. Then Wolfe and his staff loaded the train with every conceivable type of rowboat and floating craft that could be commandeered and returned to Columbus. In all, the cargo train made two trips to acquire boats for the critical rescue of cold, stranded victims. The *Dispatch* later reported that hundreds of displaced flood victims were rescued by the fleet of small boats.

A Cleveland newspaper reported on the rescue effort: "Wolfe is strong as a blacksmith and seems never to tire, and he worked with the energy of a steam engine. From his own purse he bought food for many. He paid the boatmen their fees and, when the flood was over, refused to render a bill. When the flood was over and the reckoning made of what had been done and by whom, Ohio Governor James M. Cox conferred on Robert F. Wolfe, as the law provided, the title of commodore of the Naval Reserves."

There was also a story of two heroic men whose names were unknown who lost their lives in an attempt to rescue a twelve-year-old girl from a makeshift

Newspaper publisher Robert F. Wolfe hired a special train to bring boats from Buckeye Lake to be used to rescue marooned flood victims in Columbus. *CD.*

A group of rescue volunteers mobilizes at West Town Street with boats to begin gathering marooned flood refugees. *CML.*

raft floating near Greenlawn Avenue. The men were both on horseback and fought valiantly against the current to make their way to the raft. Because this was a new experience for many, it was easy to underestimate the strength of the current. It proved too strong for them. Soon they were also overpowered and swept away by the flood currents.

William Sexton was a Columbus policeman who drowned while performing rescue duties during the flood. While helping to rescue flood victims, he fell from a rowboat in the area of Rich and Mitchell Streets. His body wasn't recovered until five days later. *CML.*

The fame of another civic hero of the day increased over the decades because of the numerous photographs of the flood carnage. On March 25, William Sexton became the fifth police officer in the history of the Columbus Police Division to lose his life in the line of duty. He was attempting to rescue flood victims from a rowboat near the intersection of Rich and Mitchell Streets when he slipped from the boat and drowned after being engulfed by the swift flood current. The police officer's body was recovered some five days later, and a photograph taken of the pool where his body surfaced was marked with an arrow. Generations of Columbus residents have revered the memory of this man because of his courage and unselfish sacrifice as they viewed and contemplated the photograph of the site where the floodwater finally gave him rest. Sexton began service as a Columbus police officer on May 1, 1905, and his badge number was 6.

The tragic deaths of Sexton and others highlight the fact that rescue was extremely dangerous and, in most cases, practically impossible, especially on Tuesday during the height of the flood. Conventional rowboats were no match for the powerful swiftness of the flood current. Relief workers were very frustrated because essentially they could do very little to help people in serious need, like Underwood with his children in the tree. However, in spite of the odds, a number of dangerous rescue attempts did succeed. Just before dark set in on Tuesday, a relief party achieved a remarkable rescue.

The team retrieved a man, a woman and a child from the roof of a house that was in motion being carried swiftly down the river. The success of the rescue was very bittersweet because the family's two additional children were drowned after they fell into the water and were lost.

Robert Oster was a chauffeur for the Murnan taxicab company and was marooned in a house throughout the night on Tuesday. He had been driving a truck that his employer loaned to the Columbus city police to transport boats and prisoners to the county jail. Oster and another driver, Paul Gyge, were caught by the floodwater in front of the workhouse on Sullivant Avenue when the levee broke. The two men stayed in the truck until it began to float away. Oster removed his shoes, placed his watch and four dollars in his mouth and began swimming to a safe house. While Oster was observing the raging floodwater and debris from the second floor of a house, he clearly saw a one-year-old child clinging to wreckage as it was being carried downstream Tuesday afternoon. Several feet behind the child was its mother, clinging to a tree. When flood wreckage struck the tree and the mother lost her grip, she went under the water and was not seen again. The child was holding on to a "raft" that its mother probably placed in the water and could be seen floating as far as the eye could reach.

People who were able to climb trees on Monday during the initial panic of the first few minutes of the flood later discovered that they were completely out of reach of any rescue boat. As the hours passed, these individuals began to suffer from hunger and exposure to cold while wearing wet clothes as they clung to the branches waiting for help. As days passed and their strength diminished, their grips loosened. Some slipped into the icy water, and currents carried their bodies downstream. In one instance, thirteen refugees had to be rescued from a single tree.

The bridges at Broad, Town and State Streets that connected the Franklinton community to the rest of Columbus were structurally compromised by the heavy currents and debris piling up until they, too, were swept away late on Tuesday morning. In addition, dozens of smaller bridges along the Scioto were very quickly washed away, leaving hundreds of people marooned in factories and mills on the west side.

The Rich Street Bridge was the only bridge to survive the powerful floodwater. Ironically, prior to the flood, the Rich Street Bridge had been condemned as unsafe and was scheduled for demolition by the presiding city administration. Not only did the bridge survive the disaster, but it was also the only escape route for thousands of refugees from Franklinton. The bridge also served as a vital lifeline for families trapped in their houses. Relief volunteers

The State Street Bridge was one of the first bridges to succumb to the strong flood currents and pileup of debris, which undermined the bridge piers and resulted in a complete collapse of the structure. *CML.*

from the east side of the river bearing supply packages from the staging center on Spring Street braved rain, snow and high winds as they steadily made their way across this remaining link to the critically disabled west side.

Since the main city bridges had been destroyed and washed away, city engineers and officials became deeply concerned about the structural integrity and safety of the railroad bridges and decided to curtail all railroad train service. The floodgates were closed for all train traffic entering or exiting Columbus on all tracks except for the Norfolk and Western line on the northeast side of town. A train locomotive on that line practically floated into Union Station at about 9:00 p.m. Tuesday night, having slogged through high waters as it made its way from Portsmouth on the Ohio River.

All of the electric service was cut off in the flooded area and in part of the downtown business section of Columbus on Tuesday night. The gas supply was also shut off to prevent explosions from broken gas lines. The city's drinking water supply was inaccessible. Refugees who had fled the flood for high ground slept in public buildings such as schools and the state hospital located on the hilltop. Members of the state militia were mobilized to assist local police in maintaining order, preventing looting and generally patrolling the streets of Columbus, which were left in total darkness.

This view is looking north from the Columbus Rich Street Bridge, which was the only downtown bridge to withstand the floodwater. *CML.*

The Columbus and Pennsylvania Railroad tracks, adjacent to Sun Manufacturing in west Columbus near the Scioto River levee. *CML.*

These flood refugees, with their baskets, are waiting to receive relief rations and clean drinking water. Columbus health officials were concerned that an outbreak of cholera could occur. *CML.*

Franklinton was totally isolated from the rest of the city and was without electric lights, phones, telegraph or any other modern means of communication. These conditions only compromised the situation further and made rescue efforts even more dangerous. However, even in the pitch-black night caused by the continued cloud cover and no moonlight, the crowd on the east side of the river continued the vigil, with anxious people peering unsuccessfully through the dark for a hopeful glimpse of a surviving family member.

Reports came in of men in rowboats looting abandoned houses in Franklinton, despite the dangers. This prompted Governor James Cox to order up the entire Ohio National Guard for duty in the flooded districts throughout the state. He declared a state of martial law for Franklinton and gave the troops strict orders to shoot anyone caught looting on sight. For three days, Governor Cox labored tirelessly from early daybreak to long past midnight, directing most of the flood relief personally for the various flood-stricken areas of Ohio, especially Dayton, Zanesville and Chillicothe.

As daylight returned on Wednesday, March 26, the generally dark scene of Franklinton's devastation was made partially visible to residents from

This scene in Columbus shows the flood debris in a yard following the water's subsidence. The subsequent cleanup required months of work throughout the community. *CML.*

other areas of Columbus community. Except for the low-lying area of Franklinton and some low areas north of Columbus near the overflow area of the Olentangy River, the balance of the city experienced the three days of torrential rain with surprisingly minor damage to property. A great sense of empathy and compassion for the victims arose among the people who were spared the flood's horror. Scores of policemen, soldiers, private citizens and city officials volunteered for flood and supply relief. The *Columbus Dispatch* and other local newspapers ran announcements listing the names of homeless survivors in the hopes that relatives elsewhere would be comforted by the news.

As officials began to collect the dead bodies, the initial estimates ranged from 100 to 150 people drowned by the floodwater. It was also estimated that well over 10,000 people from the Franklinton community were left homeless and that at least another 14,800 were living in the second-story levels and, in some cases, the attics of their homes. A severe amount of damage was done by fires on the west side during Tuesday afternoon as the floodwater snapped a number of gas lines that then somehow ignited.

Because of sustained heavy rains and the hazardous, churning floodwater, as of Wednesday evening, the rescue work was still being hindered. As if this widespread misery were not enough, the weather

This wrecked luxury automobile was a casualty of the flood. Property insurance of any kind was not a common item in 1913 for most people. Most families had to begin rebuilding their lives all over from scratch. *LOC.*

struck another cruel blow. An extremely cold Canadian air mass moved across Ohio on Wednesday night. The torrential rains now turned into icy sleet and blinding snow as the temperatures dropped sharply. These conditions were more than some people could endure, already greatly weakened by their ordeal. The sleet and snow caused fingers and toes to freeze as people clung desperately to a tree or the roofs on their partially submerged homes. It wasn't long before these people became hypothermic and frozen fingers began to lose their grip on icy surfaces, causing the demise of more victims as they slipped into the cold floodwater.

Finally, on Thursday, March 26, the floodwater began to recede, after thousands of families were forced to endure two terrible nights of rain, cold and terror. By then, it became evident that the area of Franklinton between Central and Sandusky Avenues was almost completely washed out. The casualties were very apparent to all who witnessed the aftermath of flood. One account recalled that a number of dead bodies were found huddled in the United Brethren Church on Avondale Avenue. Other bodies began washing up with the debris as the river receded. Two truckloads of human bodies were removed at one point from the west

Above: Some wood-frame homes built of quality balloon-frame construction were washed off their foundations and carried end over end downstream. Many such houses after the flood were reset on new foundations. *CML*.

Left: Samuel P. Bush was general manager of Buckeye Steel at the time of the 1913 flood and headed a relief effort to provide food, water, blankets, clothing and temporary shelter for families displaced by the flood. *CML*.

side to a morgue, where, hopefully, frantic relatives could finally identify a deceased loved one.

Hundreds of people who were still marooned on the second floors of their flooded homes were starting their second day without any food or heat in the cold March weather. Buckeye Steel general manager Samuel P. Bush (grandfather and great-grandfather of two U.S. presidents) proved to be very instrumental in organizing relief efforts. Mayor Karb appointed him chairman of the Headquarters of Relief Commission, and one of his first acts was to ask Columbus churches to take up a free will offering the following Sunday to benefit flood sufferers. A rescue effort was soon organized to free some 250 workers and flood refugees who had been trapped in the industrial facilities of the Sun Manufacturing Company on McKinley Avenue, where they had been confined since the time the levee initially failed.

Once the floodwater started receding, relief teams commenced collecting as many stranded people as could be located. A stream of the rescued men, women and children who were victims of exposure, hunger and emotional trauma were transported directly to the city hall building on State Street. Every available inch of space in the Columbus State Hospital for the Insane and Mount Carmel Hospital on the hilltop was occupied by flood refugees. Many of those rescued told eye-opening stories of split-second escapes before the waters invaded their homes, lifted the structures off foundations and crushed their homes like eggshells. The flood district between the Scioto River west bank and Sandusky Street in the central west side was cleared of both living and dead. Many flood victims from elsewhere in the state were brought to Columbus, registered at city hall and placed as refugees in private homes, public and semipublic institutions and clubs.

People who had been marooned in the business district of downtown Columbus and unable to see their families since Tuesday morning began to filter back into Franklinton on Thursday. Since the majority of the downtown bridges fell victim to the flood, people had to migrate to Dublin, Ohio, along a tedious northern route of twenty-five miles to return to the Franklinton area. Most of these people used any means of transportation available, and in some cases, they walked the entire distance to reach their homes.

Minimal civil order was restored by Friday, and many people who held vigil earlier in the week were finally reunited with their missing loved ones. Warm food and shelter were made available to the homeless. But still, many of those who had been rescued were traumatized, injured or in critical condition from the long hours they had spent during the three days and nights with no heat or food. Their clothing had been drenched by incessant rain and sleet, and many were still shivering and wearing blank expressions on their faces. These people were a piteous sight. Some could barely stand on their feet. Others were shaking so violently from the numbing cold that they could hardly be helped into the waiting boats.

Rail transportation services slowly resumed in areas where the floodwater could be drained. Utility linemen began resetting poles and

A woman looks from a second-floor window, as she is marooned and isolated until the floodwater subsides. *LOC.*

Once the Franklinton levee failed, the employees of Sun Manufacturing became trapped inside for three days until they were rescued by volunteers with boats. *CML.*

Chicago Avenue in the Franklinton area of west Columbus. These automobiles were washed more than one mile from where they were originally parked. *CML.*

This high-riding horse-drawn wagon provided the perfect means of transportation through floodwater for this Columbus family. *CML.*

hanging new wire and cables to reestablish telephone and telegraph service. Governor Cox turned his attention to the dangers of diseases and epidemics, such as cholera. A "boil water order" was issued to the public in regard to their drinking water. Scenes of tragedy were everywhere. The bloated, decaying carcasses of hundreds of unfortunate animals littered the streets, creating an obstacle course in the flooded area along with a heavy putrid stench. Dismembered bodies of people who were disfigured beyond recognition were being dug out of the debris.

On Saturday, March 29, a strange and unexpected event occurred. About one thousand people, refugees from the Dayton, Ohio flood calamity, arrived in Columbus seeking relief from that community's tremendous ordeal. Most of them had made their way to the seat of their state government in Model T–type cars or by train. They wanted help from their elected officials, but the Dayton refugees soon discovered that the devastation in Columbus was nearly as bad as the conditions they had just left behind. While no arrangements had been made to care for these additional people, the relief teams rationed their resources to be able to provide for the newcomers.

Between Tuesday morning and Saturday, about one hundred babies were born in the difficult conditions of the flood district and in the refugee camps. In one awkward situation, a woman known only as Mrs. Olmstead gave birth while being tossed about in a frail rescue boat. The child was born midway between the place of rescue and the landing at the Rich Street Bridge. Upon landing, a patrolman name Edward E. Shaw wrapped the newborn in his overcoat and transported mother and child to a private home. In most cases, neither mothers nor the newborn babies received any medical attention, and in some cases, a few infants soon died of exposure. Four of the babies were reported to have been born in a school on the hilltop. One child was named "Dana Rose" after the Dana Elementary School, which sheltered her mother during this time of horror.

In an emotional speech given on the evening of Sunday, March 30, just shortly before he left his office at the statehouse for home and the first full night of sleep in over a week, Governor Cox delivered this statement:

Opposite, top: Some one thousand refugees from Dayton, Ohio, arrived in Columbus seeking relief from that community's tremendous flood ordeal. *CML.*

Opposite, bottom: About one hundred babies were born in the difficult conditions of the Columbus flood district and in the local refugee camps. *CML.*

WANTED

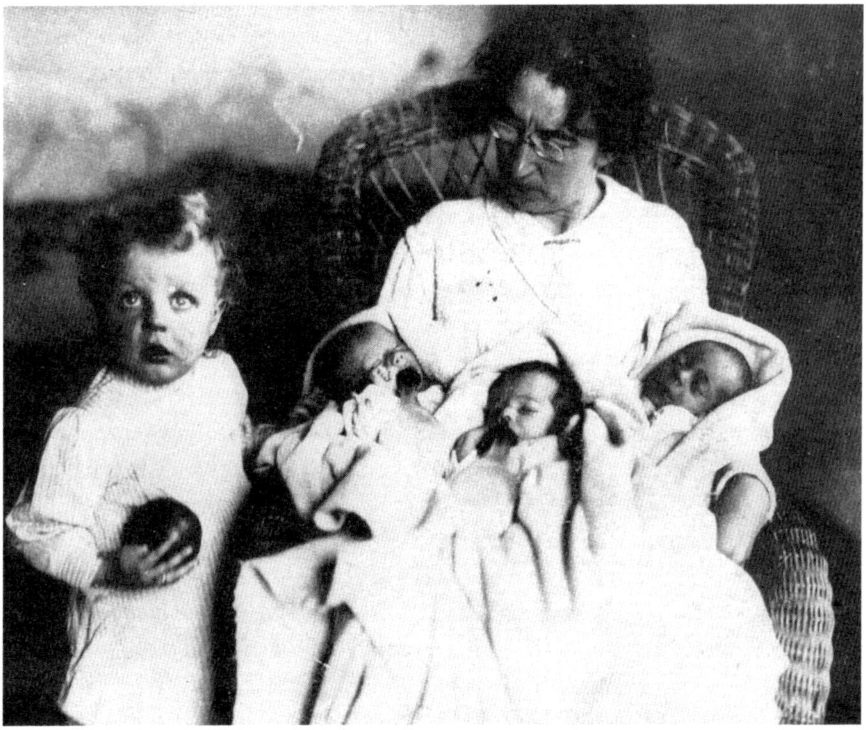

> *Refreshed by the tears of American people, Ohio stands ready from today to meet the crisis alone. Ohio has risen from the floods. Such a pitiless blow from Nature as we sustained would have wiped out society and destroyed governments in other days. We cannot speak our gratitude to President Wilson for federal aid, to the Red Cross, to state, municipalities, trade organizations and individuals that sent funds and supplies. They will never know their contribution to humanity.*
>
> *The relief situation, so far as food and clothing are concerned, is in hand. Thankful to her friends who succored her, Ohio faces tomorrow serene and confident.*

This was the sobering situation Sunday evening exactly one week after three killer air masses collided on the morning of Easter Sunday in 1913. The flood left behind widespread misery, destruction and death. What did the people who survived this calamity remember most about the flood? One Columbus man recalled that his grandparents were swept downstream along with their house. He never saw them alive again, and sometime later, their bodies were finally recovered in Portsmouth, Ohio, about eighty miles south of Columbus, where the Scioto River empties into the Ohio River.

Everyone in the community had private memories of horror and sorrow, but there were a few basic facts that were common to all who witnessed the flood. One was that the entire city of Columbus lost its drinking water supply for twenty hours because the Scioto River pumping station had to be taken out of service. Also, the Franklinton area did not regain its water service until a week later. All Columbus public schools were closed for three days, and the nine public schools located in Franklinton were closed for five weeks or more. The children who attended those schools were temporarily transferred to other school buildings until the flooded buildings could be dried out and cleaned. Streetcar service was temporarily suspended all over Columbus, and tram service did not resume in Franklinton for nearly thirty days. Many of the streets in Franklinton were so clogged with dead animals and flood debris that normal traffic was impossible, and the danger of disease was great. Because the flood had done extensive damage to the tracks, railroad service had to be curtailed for weeks.

Regarding just Columbus, 4.2 square miles of the city—occupied by a population of twenty-seven thousand—was flooded by the Easter Sunday storms that caused the west bank levee of the Scioto River to break. The Great Flood of 1913 stands alone as the largest and most tragic disaster experienced by the people of Columbus. The public soon reached a point where people insisted on having a permanent solution to the area flooding. The Columbus City Council gave Mayor Karb and Samuel Kinnear, director of public works, the authority to secure the services of a capable engineering firm that was thoroughly familiar with hydraulics to perform a study and make a report on the best alternatives for alleviating the local flood problem associated with the Scioto and Olentangy Rivers. On April 8, 1913, Chicago engineers John W. Alvord and Charles B. Burdick were selected to prepare the study. At the conclusion of the study in September, ten different projects were presented. Only two were recommended, both of which would cost, according to the estimates, more than $11 million. The first project proposed abandoning the old river channel around the bend and cutting a new channel to take the total flow across the west side between McDowell and Skidmore Streets.

John Alvord was a hydraulics engineer very familiar with the storm water conditions in central Ohio. His firm conducted an in-depth investigation of local conditions and prepared a report for Columbus City officials with recommendations for extensive flood control projects. *PC.*

The second project proposed building water detention reservoirs above Dublin and Delaware and substituting a new, straight channel for the older, crooked channel. This project called for the construction of what would become years later the O'Shaughnessy Dam and reservoir north of Dublin, which also would greatly increase the drinking water supply for central Ohio. Also, decades later, a dam and a 963-acre reservoir were constructed just north of Delaware, Ohio.

After spirited discussions in and out of the public press, it was estimated that the city's initial share of the capital improvements by the first favored plan would be $8.5 million. The question of funding was submitted for a vote to the people, who viewed building a new channel as too radical, and the issue was overwhelmingly defeated. The following March, the Ohio General Assembly passed the Vonderheide Act, creating flood conservancy districts, each with a board to be appointed by a panel of county common pleas judges. The Central Ohio Conservancy Board was instructed to prepare plans for flood control that, after approval by the judges, were to be executed by the conservancy district. For the central Ohio district, Julius F. Stone, George W. Lattimer and George E. Williams were appointed, and they quickly employed the same engineering firm that created the report for the city of Columbus. After a more thorough study by Alvord and Burdick, it was also determined that the plan of detention reservoirs, combined with channel improvements, would afford protection not only to Columbus but also to the district north as far as Delaware and south as far as Chillicothe. This prompted an effort to enlarge the district, but it failed.

It then appeared that the whole cost would have to be assessed on Franklin County. This was regarded as such a costly project that many felt it would amount to just confiscating property in the flood district that was already substantially depreciated. The conservancy board was split on this proposition, so the plan was presented to the judges and was disapproved. Then began a movement to ignore the conservancy board and have the channel improvements paid for by the City of Columbus alone. The Columbus city engineer was asked to make an estimate for the cost of a 580-foot channel, twice the width of the old channel. The first estimate showed that it could be done for $5 million. The council directed the preparation of plans for a project that could be executed for $3.5 million. Once this was done, a bond issue in that amount was put on the ballot for the November 1916 election. The public voted to approve the proposition by a large margin.

Next, the necessary property was appraised and acquired by eminent domain. The project contracts were awarded, and the work of channel widening began in April under the direction of R.H. Simpson, of the Columbus city engineering division. By August 1918, about $500,000 had been spent in acquiring the needed ground and $250,000 in project contracts. With three-fourths of the first $1 million used, the federal government authorized the issue of a second $1 million as a wartime necessity during World War I. With this acquisition, the city now owned every foot of the west bank of the Scioto from the mouth of the Olentangy south to the sewage disposal plant and all on the east side for the same distance. An earthen levee was then constructed along the west bank, except for a distance 1,200 feet north of Broad Street, where concrete was used.

A Plan to Divert the Scioto River is the title of this drawing by artist Billy Ireland for the *Columbus Evening Dispatch*. *CD*.

The flood control project that Columbus initially decided to implement was "project number 7" of the ten proposals submitted by Alvord and Burdick. The following is a brief description of that plan, which provided for a maximum storm and runoff channel flow of 150,000 cubic feet per second. This flow rate included a factor of safety that would allow about one half more flow before overtopping the levees. From the mouth of the Olentangy, where the two rivers converge, the flow would be carried south through a new channel called the May Street Cutoff and rejoin the Scioto

River again just below Mound Street. The present bed of the Scioto River around the bend to Mound Street was to be abandoned, filled and made into a park or boulevard. The following brief account gives the key features of the project that were never fully implemented:

> *FLOOD WATER ELEVATION: The maximum water height is proposed to allow the flood water to rise while carrying the above described amount of flow at a level much lower than that produced in the flood of March 1913 in the city. This lower height is obtained largely by the fact that adequate and direct outlet is obtained through the west side, and in part by depth and width of the new channel.*
>
> *NEW MAY STREET CHANNEL: The new channel across the west side will be centered along the line of May Street and will be about 880 feet wide at the top. The east line will be along McDowell Street, and the west line along Skidmore Street. The height of these streets will be raised from ten to eighteen feet above the present level. On both sides of the channel it will be necessary to condemn a strip of from one to two blocks in width. This is in order to grade the slopes up to the new level. It is proposed, in the future, to make a park out of these two strips of land after they have been filled. About 750 buildings will need to be condemned and removed. The sides of the channel will be sloped and sodded, and a level bench about 30 feet wide will be formed just above the low water pool. The width of the low water channel will be about 600 feet, and the water level held by the dam under the Mound Street Bridge will be about twenty feet above city base line elevation or datum. The bottom of the channel will be twelve feet above city datum, giving a depth at low water of eight feet.*
>
> *EXCAVATION: The largest part of the excavation for the project was to be taken from the May Street cutoff channel. The largest portion of this excavated material will be used for filling the old river bed around the Bend.*
>
> *LEVEES: In order to protect the northerly line of the Franklinton area, a massive new levee would be constructed along the Scioto River. This levee is to have a top width of 100 feet, and a height of twelve feet above the high water mark of the design flood elevation. It will terminate at the west end in the higher ground near the State Asylum, and at Sandusky Street it will connect with an elevated parkway along the west side of the new May Street cutoff channel. Along the east side of the new May Street cutoff channel a new avenue will be opened, on a raised grade, which will pass from Dublin Avenue or Spring Street west of the Hocking Valley Railroad straight south to Mound Street. This will provide a new and important*

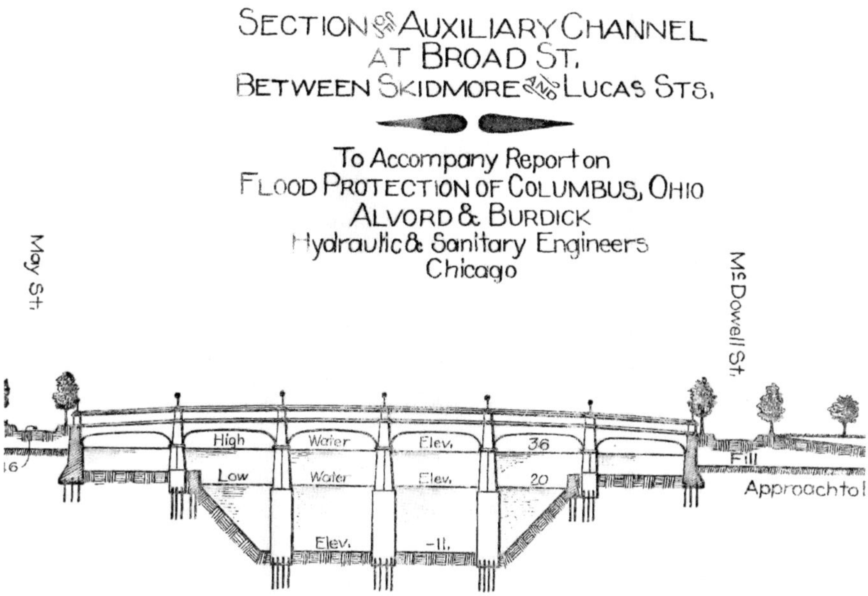

An engineer's proposed concept for increasing the floodwater capacity of the Scioto River at Broad Street. *CDW.*

thoroughfare for connecting the West Side with both the north and the south sides of the city. A third levee of importance will run north along the east side of the Olentangy bottoms to the high ground in the vicinity of Third Avenue. This will protect the district north of the Penitentiary from being engulfed by flood waters. This latter levee will be eighty feet in width, and of a sufficient height to be safe against all accidental ice gorges or other unusual conditions.

THE OLENTANGY RIVER: It is proposed to buy about 540 acres of bottom land up the Olentangy valley as far as Dodridge Street Bridge, so that no encroachment of subdivision or building operations shall be made upon the flood water channel of the river. Nearly all of the street bridges on the Olentangy will require some enlargement of their water-way opening. A levee east of the Olentangy River will be constructed to protect the region north of Spring Street and west of Neil Avenue. The railroad bridges crossing the Olentangy River near its mouth will all require some enlargement and alteration in order to give this channel the effective capacity.

THE SCIOTO RIVER BELOW THE MOUND STREET BRIDGE: It is proposed that a levee be built to connect Mound Street with Jackson Pike in the

This is a temporary bridge structure under construction over the Scioto River. This was built to serve as the Broad Street Bridge from 1913 until 1921. *CML.*

vicinity of Greenlawn Avenue. This levee will have a substantial width so that it may be converted into a thoroughfare in the future if desired. The east levee below Mound Street will pass around the Franklin Iron Works and then south-easterly to the old canal bed and the high ground at a point north of the Greenlawn Avenue Bridge where the levee will terminate. Below this point the flood plain of the river will be used as it originally existed. It is proposed that the city shall acquire all of the land below Mound Street to a point just below the Sewage Treatment Plant from the old canal right-of-way on the east side to the rising ground at the Jackson Pike on the west side. This land will comprise about 1,620 acres. The levees around the Sewage Pumping Station and the Sewage Treatment Plant are to be raised and reinforced, but these public work facilities are not to be disturbed otherwise. The old levees immediately along the Scioto River below Mound Street will be kept in place in order as a defense measure against ordinary floods. The extraordinary floods which will be expected to overtop the old levees will be confined by the larger levees and the broader flood plain called for in the improvements.

The Local Fear of a Dam Break

A frenzy of panic and terror filled Columbus at about 4:30 p.m. on Wednesday, March 26, 1913, as a rumor began to spread that the Scioto River storage dam had failed due to the flooding and burst open. At any time, a huge body of water would sweep into downtown Columbus. The rumor was passed around by word of mouth and by telephone until the entire community was in fear for their lives.

Franklinton, which is on the west side of the Scioto River, was already underwater from a gigantic flood that had killed more than ninety-six people just days before. The press had reported that dead bodies were lodged in trees and that cemetery coffins were unearthed, as well as provided detailed descriptions of all sorts of flood horrors over the past forty-eight hours. The prospect of a wall of water rushing down the swollen river struck fear in the general population of downtown Columbus just across the river from the devastation and where people were, for the most part, unaffected by the flood. But once the rumor took hold, thousands of people believed that it was the end of their world. Stores in the downtown area were completely deserted, and people were fainting from fear and exhaustion. Hundreds ran to the dome of the state capitol building and jammed the steps to the cupola in search of a higher perch for safety. Police and militiamen rushed into stores and office buildings, spreading the unfounded warning and adding to the confusion and terrific fear that had completely captured the downtown area. Thousands of men and women, young and old, professionals, clericals and tradesmen, took to the streets on foot and started running. Women were trying desperately to lead their sobbing children to safety as both stumbled, paralyzed with fear. Horses released from stables ran through downtown, adding more confusion to the tumultuous crowd of people, vehicles, wagons and assorted domestic animals.

When no water rushed in, people gradually determined that it was a false alarm. The next day's newspaper reported that if the dam had completely failed (according to Charles Hoover's calculations), it would have only added an extra two inches to the actual floodwater. City engineer Julian Griggs and James Westwater, the general contractor who constructed the dam, were both quoted in the newspaper the following day as stating, "The dam cannot break, and if it did it would not cause any additional damage." Unlike Johnstown's dam, which was an earthen dam, the Scioto storage dam was made of steel-reinforced concrete and anchored in a trench made of solid stone that was six to eight feet deep. During the high-water mark of the flood, the water was nearly twelve feet above the crest of the dam. Additionally, the abutment ends were fifty-two feet high because the dam was designed and constructed to subsequently have an additional twenty feet in height added to increase the city's supply of raw river water. At no time was there any danger of a dam failure. Apparently, the design engineers had designed the dam with the tragedy of the Johnstown flood in mind, showing they had learned a lesson from past events.

Columbus native James Grover Thurber was an author and cartoonist who for a time worked for the *Columbus Dispatch*. In 1933, he wrote about his life in Columbus in a book titled *My Life and Hard Times*. In the third chapter, he recalled his family's experience during the flood in 1913, when he was eighteen years old. Thurber used the flood incident as the basis for a short story "The Day the Dam Broke" (also the name of the chapter). Using his classic wit, he described the fear and panic that overtook downtown Columbus when the rumor that the water storage dam had collapsed as a result of the floodwater getting out of control:

> *My memories of what my family and I went through during the 1913 flood in Ohio I would gladly forget. And yet neither the hardships we endured nor the turmoil and confusion we experienced can alter my feeling toward my native state and city. I am having a fine time now and wish Columbus were here, but if anyone ever wished a city was in hell it was during that frightful and perilous afternoon in 1913 when the dam broke, or, to be more exact, when everybody in town thought that the dam broke. We were both ennobled and demoralized by the experience. Grandfather especially*

This drawing by James Thurber depicts two thousand Columbus citizens panicking and running east because of a rumor that the Scioto River dam was about to break and flood the downtown area. *CH.*

rose to magnificent heights which can never lose their splendor for me, even though his reactions to the flood were based upon a profound misconception; namely, that Nathan Bedford Forrest's cavalry was the menace we were called upon to face. The only possible means of escape for us was to flee the house, a step which grandfather sternly forbade, brandishing his old army saber in his hand. "Let the sons -- ------- come!" he roared. Meanwhile hundreds of people were streaming by our house in wild panic, screaming "Go east! Go east!" We had to stun grandfather with the ironing board. Impeded as we were by the inert form of the old gentleman—he was taller than six feet and weighed almost a hundred and seventy pounds—we were passed, in the first half-mile, by practically everybody else in the city. Had grandfather not come to, at the corner of Parsons Avenue and Town Street, we would unquestionably have been overtaken and engulfed by the roaring waters—that is, if there had been any roaring waters. Later, when the panic had died down and people had gone rather sheepishly back to their homes and their offices, minimizing the distances they had run and offering various reasons for running, city engineers pointed out that even if the dam had broken, the water level would not have risen more than two additional inches in the West Side. The West Side was, at the time of the dam scare, under thirty feet of water—as, indeed, were all Ohio river towns during the great spring floods of twenty years ago. The East Side (where we lived and where all the running occurred) had never been in any danger at all. Only a rise of some ninety-five feet could have caused the flood waters to flow over High Street—the thoroughfare that divided the east side of town from the west—and engulf the East Side.

The fact that we were all as safe as kittens under a cook stove did not, however, assuage in the least the fine despair and the grotesque desperation which seized upon the residents of the East Side when the cry spread like a grass fire that the dam had given way. Some of the most dignified, staid, cynical, and clear-thinking men in town abandoned their wives, stenographers, homes, and offices and ran east. There are few alarms in the world more terrifying than "The dam has broken!" There are few persons capable of stopping to reason when that clarion cry strikes upon their ears, even persons who live in towns no nearer than five hundred miles to a dam.

The Columbus, Ohio, broken-dam rumor began, as I recall it, about noon of March 12, 1913. High Street, the main canyon of trade, was loud with the placid hum of business and the buzzing of placid businessmen arguing, computing, wheedling, offering, refusing, compromising. Darius Conningway, one of the foremost corporation lawyers in the Middle-West, was telling the Public Utilities Commission in the language of Julius Caesar that they might as well try to move the Northern star as to move him. Other men were making their little boasts and their little gestures. Suddenly somebody began to run. It may be that he had simply remembered, all of a moment, an engagement to meet his wife, for which he was now frightfully late. Whatever it was, he ran east on Broad Street (probably toward the Maramor Restaurant, a favorite place for a man to meet his wife). Somebody else began to run, perhaps a newsboy in high spirits. Another man, a portly gentleman of affairs, broke into a trot. Inside of ten minutes, everybody on High Street, from the Union Depot to the Courthouse, was running. A loud mumble gradually crystallized into the dread word "dam." "The dam has broke!" The fear was put into words by a little old lady in an electric, or by a traffic cop, or by a small boy: nobody knows who, nor does it now really matter. Two thousand people were abruptly in full flight. "Go east!," was the cry that arose—east away from the river, east to safety. "Go east! Go east! Go east!"

Black streams of people flowed eastward down all the streets leading in that direction; these streams, whose headwaters were in the dry goods stores, office buildings, harness shops, movie theatres, were fed by trickles of housewives, children, cripples, servants, dogs, and cats, slipping out of the houses past which the main streams flowed, shouting and screaming. People ran out leaving fires burning and food cooking and doors wide open. I remember, however, that my mother turned out all the fires and that she took with her a dozen eggs and two loaves of bread. It was her plan to make Memorial Hall, just two blocks away, and take refuge somewhere in the top of it, in one of the dusty rooms where war veterans met and where old battle flags and stage scenery were stored. But the seething throngs, shouting "Go east!" drew her along and the rest of us with her. When grandfather regained full consciousness, at Parsons Avenue, he turned upon the retreating mob like a vengeful prophet and exhorted the men to form ranks and stand off the Rebel dogs, but at length he, too, got the idea that the dam had broken and, roaring "Go east!" in his powerful voice, he caught up in one arm a small child and in the other a slight clerkish man of perhaps forty-two and we slowly began to gain on those ahead of us.

A scattering of firemen, policemen, and army officers in dress uniforms—there had been a review at Fort Hayes, in the northern part of town—added color to the surging billows of people. "Go east!" cried a little child in a piping voice, as she ran past a porch on which drowsed a lieutenant-colonel of infantry. Used to quick decisions, trained to immediate obedience, the officer bounded off the porch and, running at full tilt, soon passed the child, bawling "Go east!" The two of them emptied rapidly the houses of the little street they were on. "What is it? What is it?" demanded a fat, waddling man who intercepted the colonel. The officer dropped behind and asked the little child what it was. "The dam has broke!" gasped the girl. "The dam has broke!" roared the colonel. "Go east! Go east! Go east!" He was soon leading, with the exhausted child in his arms, a fleeing company of three hundred persons who had gathered around him from living-rooms, shops, garages, backyards, and basements.

Nobody has ever been able to compute with any exactness how many people took part in the great rout of 1913, for the panic, which extended from the Winslow Bottling Works in the south end to Clintonville, six miles north, ended as abruptly as it began and the bobtail and ragtag and velvet-gowned groups of refugees melted away and slunk home, leaving the streets peaceful and deserted. The shouting, weeping, tangled evacuation of the city lasted not more than two hours in all. Some few people got as far east as Reynoldsburg, twelve miles away; fifty or more reached the Country Club, eight miles away; most of the others gave up, exhausted, or climbed trees in Franklin Park, four miles out. Order was restored and fear dispelled finally by means of militiamen riding about in motor lorries bawling through megaphones: "The dam has not broken!" At first this tended only to add to the confusion and increase the panic, for many stampeders thought the soldiers were bellowing "The dam has now broken!," thus setting an official seal of authentication on the calamity.

"It's got us!" he shouted.

All the time, the sun shone quietly and there was nowhere any sign of oncoming waters. A visitor in an airplane, looking down on the straggling, agitated masses of people below, would have been hard put to it to divine a reason for the phenomenon. It must have inspired, in such an observer, a peculiar kind of terror, like the sight of the Marie Celeste, abandoned at sea, its galley fires peacefully burning, and its tranquil decks bright in the sunlight.

An aunt of mine, Aunt Edith Taylor, was in a movie theatre on High Street when, over and above the sound of the piano in the pit (a W.S. Hart picture was being shown), there rose the steadily increasing tromp of running feet. Persistent shouts rose above the tromping. An elderly man, sitting near my aunt, mumbled something, got out of his seat, and went up the aisle at a dogtrot. This started everybody. In an instant the audience was jamming the aisles. "Fire!" shouted a woman who always expected to be burned up in a theatre; but now the shouts outside were louder and coherent. "The dam has broke!" cried somebody. "Go east!" screamed a small woman in front of my aunt. And east they went, pushing and shoving and clawing, knocking women and children down, emerging finally into the street, torn and sprawling. Inside the theatre, Bill Hart was calmly calling some desperado's bluff and the brave girl at the piano played "Row! Row! Row!" loudly and then "In My Harem." Outside, men were streaming across the Statehouse yard, others were climbing trees, a woman managed to get up onto the "These Are My Jewels" statue, whose bronze figures of Sherman, Stanton, Grant, and Sheridan watched with cold unconcern the going to pieces of the capital city.

"I ran south to State Street, east on State to Third, south on Third to Town, and out east on Town," my Aunt Edith has written me. "A tall spare woman with grim eyes and a determined chin ran past me down the middle of the street. I was still uncertain as to what was the matter, in spite of all the shouting. I drew up alongside the woman with some effort, for

although she was in her late fifties, she had a beautiful easy running form and seemed to be in excellent condition. 'What is it?' I puffed. She gave me a quick glance and then looked ahead again, stepping up her pace a trifle. 'Don't ask me, ask God!' she said.

"When I reached Grant Avenue, I was so spent that Dr. H.R. Mallory—you remember Dr. Mallory, the man with the white beard who looks like Robert Browning?—well, Dr. Mallory, whom I had drawn away from at the corner of Fifth and Town, passed me. 'It's got us!' he shouted, and I felt sure that whatever it was did have us, for you know what conviction Dr. Mallory's statements always carried. I didn't know at the time what he meant, but I found out later. There was a boy behind him on roller-skates, and Dr. Mallory mistook the swishing of the skates for the sound of rushing water. He eventually reached the Columbus School for Girls, at the corner of Parsons Avenue and Town Street, where he collapsed, expecting the cold frothing waters of the Scioto to sweep him into oblivion. The boy on the skates swirled past him and Dr. Mallory realized for the first time what he had been running from. Looking back up the street, he could see no signs of water, but nevertheless, after resting a few minutes, he jogged on east again. He caught up with me at Ohio Avenue, where we rested together. I should say that about seven hundred people passed us. A funny thing was that all of them were on foot. Nobody seemed to have had the courage to stop and start his car; but as I remember it, all cars had to be cranked in those days, which is probably the reason."

The next day, the city went about its business as if nothing had happened, but there was no joking. It was two years or more before you dared treat the breaking of the dam lightly. And even now, twenty years after, there are a few persons, like Dr. Mallory, who will shut up like a clam if you mention the Afternoon of the Great Run.

Statewide Communication Failure and Restoration

The wide extent of death and destruction throughout the state of Ohio and beyond during the Great Flood of 1913 exceeded all other weather events in Ohio history to that date and consequently justified the moniker of "Ohio's greatest natural disaster." Torrential rainfall blanketed the entire state with well over six to eleven inches of rain, and every area of the state was in some way affected. At least 460 people died during the flood. The estimate of just residential houses that were totally destroyed exceeded 39,500 structures. When the flood was over, Ohioans began to assess the damage. Property damage was extensive, as many other homes were seriously damaged. Factories, railroads and some other structures were completely lost. In some parts of the state, officials chose to dynamite canal locks in an attempt to alleviate flooding. By the early twentieth century, few canals were still in operation in Ohio, but the destruction of the locks ensured the permanent end to the era of canal transportation in Ohio history.

Downstream along the Miami River, there were more than one hundred deaths in Hamilton, Ohio, where the floodwater ranged from ten to eighteen feet deep in some residential neighborhoods. As mentioned previously, there were ninety-six deaths in Columbus alone when the Scioto River reached record levels and emptied water that ran nine to seventeen feet deep through the streets of the near west side. Many Columbus residents quickly escaped to the safety of rooftops and trees. The Columbus floodwater ran swiftly downstream to Circleville and on to Chillicothe, where practically the entire low-lying community was under water.

Rear view of Cincinnati's Grand Central Railroad Depot during high floodwater. *LOC.*

For a number of days in Cincinnati and many cities in the Midwest, shuttling by boat was the only practical means of transportation through low-lying neighborhoods. *LOC.*

Cincinnati's flooded riverfront and downtown district, looking from the direction of Newport, Kentucky, with the Roebling Bridge in the foreground. *LOC.*

In Zanesville, the Muskingum River crested twenty-seven feet above general flood stage, and water was as much as twenty feet deep at several downtown intersections. On the famous Y-bridge, the street lampposts were barely visible. In Defiance, the Maumee River crested ten feet above flood stage, and 268 homes were submerged in floodwater. As in Columbus, many people were rescued from rooftops and trees. In Tiffin, Ohio, nineteen died when their homes were washed off their foundations and collapsed into the Sandusky River. In Cleveland, the floodwater of the Cuyahoga River washed away docks, lumberyards, trains and railroad yards. Seven locks on the Ohio Canal at Akron had to be dynamited to allow the floodwater to drain back into the Cuyahoga River. The levees along the Ohio River at Portsmouth were topped, causing the flooding of 4,500 homes. The surface of the Ohio River at Cincinnati rose twenty-one feet in twenty-four hours.

A frequent and immediate consequence of any natural disaster is the loss of communication services, such as telephone and telegraph in the case of the 1913 flood. When these vital services are shut off for any reason, the ability to coordinate rescue planning, supply relief, volunteer assembly and any amount of remedial efforts is severely compromised. The inability of loved ones to contact other family members, especially for the purpose of issuing a careful warning of impending danger, only increases the horror, fear, pain and calamity we tend to associate with natural disasters. Many utility services such as water, gas and electricity were rendered inoperable by the floodwater. It is interesting to realize that once these vital services were curtailed, the main element of human interaction that was required to restore service was a reliable means for a multitude of workers, coordinators, suppliers and volunteers to communicate repeatedly.

Until the breakup of the telephone monopolies in the late twentieth century, much of the Midwest received telephone service via the American Telephone and Telegraph Company (AT&T) and its numerous affiliates. In looking at the calamity of the great flood, we often marginalize the colossal behind-the-scenes achievements of the common working individuals whose dedication to serving the public often goes unsung and unnoticed. For this reason, it would be fitting to take a much closer look at the way in which the terrible flood affected the public's ability to communicate via telephone. A spotlight will also be focused on how, through sheer human effort and ingenuity, the telephone system that was destroyed in some places was quickly restored to service and kept alive to serve the efforts of rescue and flood relief.

On March 23, following three days of rainstorms, a Bell System employee (whose name happened to be John Bell) sent out a distress call to initiate relief forces from every quarter to aid those in peril in flood-deluged and fire-ravaged Dayton, Ohio. John Bell's message was sent after the culmination of a series of disasters that made 1913 a notable year in the history of the American Telephone and Telegraph Company, whose wires had been swept by rainstorms of unparalleled severity throughout the territory between the Rocky Mountains and the eastern Alleghenies. Service trouble began one month before the March storms when, on February 22, a sleet storm disabled transmission wires over a wide expanse of territory. In the Chicago exchange, one by one the lines went out, and by 3:00 p.m., Chicago had lost telephone communication with Milwaukee. In its fury, the rainstorm tore down the main pole lead of the entire system for a distance of about sixteen city blocks, and hundreds of wires snapped beneath their weighty coating of ice and the onslaught of gale winds.

In a remarkably short time, though, a temporary service was installed, and communication service was restored. The work of returning the lines to permanent shape was started as soon as the ice was off the wires and was progressing rapidly when another storm swept down from the northwest on March 21. Both the new and temporary work were ripped from their fastenings and torn into pieces, causing the splintering and uprooting of more than 5,500 poles belonging to AT&T and its subsidiaries. Once again, Chicago was cut off from wire communication with other points, although not completely. While these conditions were at their worst, a detoured message via Denver and Kansas City came to the Chicago office telling of a series of terrible tornados that had torn across Omaha's finest neighborhood and business section. The aftermath was described as a fearful, jagged wound, littered with the wreckage of buildings that had buried a number of human beings. The country stood shocked at the ruin that had been wrought by the twister. But at the same time, the public was very anxious and fearful to hear further details of the tragedy. Again by superhuman effort, the telephone lines were reopened, but even as the fearsome tales were flying over the wires, the lines to the east of Chicago were suddenly lost, and rumors came of a calamity that made the country shudder.

Heavy and incessant rains had been falling throughout the Ohio and Indiana region, beginning the night of March 21, the Friday before Easter. From an area of land that extended in a southeasterly direction across Ohio from Trumbull to Drake County, the waters of the Muskingum, Scioto and Miami Rivers and their tributaries moved swiftly. Altogether, these major streams made up the drainage system of about 80 percent of Ohio. The rainfall at the headwaters of these streams ran up to the unprecedented figures of seven to eight inches of rain in the forty-eight hours before the flood. This brought the water up to the top of the banks and levees, where it paused just for a moment before unleashing itself on unsuspecting people. The floods engulfed Columbus, Dayton, Chillicothe, Zanesville, Indianapolis, Terre Haute, Muncie and a score of smaller towns in a swirling, seething flood of mud and water that carried death and destruction in its path. The torrent of water overturned houses, uprooted trees, threw railroad tracks like they were soda straws far from their roadbeds and poured ruthlessly through storefronts and factories. The water, mud and debris plunged one of the fairest sections of Midwestern America into chaos and darkness, with no chance to cry out to the waiting world and tell the story of its suffering and horror.

Given the obstacles that the weather presented, especially in regard to transportation, there appeared to be absolutely no chance of reestablishing telephone service until the rain stopped and the water receded. But one highly determined "telephone man" found the way to send news of the dire calamity that had brought Dayton to the place where it was fighting for its life. The man, surrounded by floodwater, pelted by rain and snow, hungry, waterlogged and working in the dark, climbed alone to the roof

Telegraph and telephone utility poles were hampered by the weight of ice and were often knocked down by large floating debris such as whole houses, farm sheds and railroad cars. *LOC.*

of the Main Exchange of the Central Union Telephone Company in Dayton. Using only his testing set, this clever technician managed to open communication with the village of Phoneton some eight miles to the north. Then the world learned that a catastrophe had fallen on the industrial community and that serious help must come and come quickly. Warm hearts and eager hands throughout the land flew into action to offer assistance. Very soon, that serious help and supplies were en route over quaking railroads, tottering bridges and dark, miry roads to aid Dayton. This was made possible by a "telephone man" who was spartan in his courage, forgetful of self while defying hunger, dampness and cold to reestablish communication with the outside world. This man stayed at that post to tell the listening world of the happenings and desperate needs in the flood-bound city of Dayton. No ancient bridge famed in legend was more tenaciously held than was that telephone line from Dayton to Phoneton by John Bell, "telephone man."

All the while Bell was securing Dayton's communication with the rest of the world, at Columbus another man of the hour was making history. As the floodwater raged over the Franklinton area of west Columbus, Wire Chief Tom Green was at the long-distance test board, tracing out new routes by which word could be sent and received by the various isolated communities that were fearfully in a panic and calling for aid. For hours upon hours, Green stood firm, and when phone lines were swept away in one direction, he worked out new routes to take their place and maintain critically needed open lines of communication. The effectiveness of Ohio's civil authority had to be bolstered to provide help and protect the citizens of Dayton in their time of misfortune. The ability of Governor Cox to issue effective orders and initiate action, such as mobilizing the militia, depended on the ability of Green to pass the word over the wires. The relief work had to be an organized effort, and Tom Green was determined to see that the plans were conveyed to all concerned parties.

Green's vigil during the 1913 flood began when he went to work early on March 25. He had anticipated trouble on the long-distance lines because of the heavy rains. He was performing routine testing on a line running to the Marion, Ohio vicinity when someone broke in on him. It was the manager of the local telephone company at La Rue, in Marion County, Ohio, some forty miles due north of Columbus. He was calling to say that the citizens of that village were driven to the second stories of buildings and homes because of high water. "We must have help or we'll be wiped off the map" was the startling appeal made to Wire Chief Green. At that moment, scores of wires in all parts of Ohio transmitted the same plea for assistance. Green transferred the La Rue dilemma directly to the governor's mansion, which routed Governor Cox out of bed to tell him of the trouble. Green began to brief the governor on how boats should be secured at the Lewiston reservoir because no other boats were available. Green knew this because earlier he had been in communication with a dozen relief committees that might be in a position to give help. As it turned out, very few boats could be spared since they were needed for use in their own flooded districts.

Not long after the wire chief advised the governor of La Rue's trouble and of reported dangerously high water in other parts of the state, other public officials woke up to this situation—unique in regard to the state's previous flood experience and the generation in current leadership. The havoc was not confined to a single community, as had been the case with the Johnstown, Pennsylvania flood in 1889 and the recent San Francisco earthquake and fire. This tragedy was taking a toll over half of the state and beyond. Thanks to the prompt action of Governor Cox and Wire Chief Green, the damage in La Rue was minimized.

A new Columbus city fire engine from Engine House No. 10 was overturned and destroyed during the flood. *CML.*

The high floodwater of the White River between Anderson and Muncie, Indiana, caused havoc as they washed out entire railroad bridges and roads. *LOC.*

Throughout the state, though, railroad transportation was almost completely paralyzed. Trains were stalled and delayed, and at one point, all rail traffic came to a standstill for more than forty-eight hours. As bridges were washed out and steel rails were carried from the roadbed and into streams by the floodwater, the telegraph and telephone poles and miles upon miles of wire often became entangled with the wreckage. Railroad officers, engineers, mechanics and trackmen worked in defiance of sleep, day and night, to restore rail service to stricken communities. Telegraph and telephone companies, through loyal, hardworking employees, labored feverishly to get the poles in place and wires returned to service. Transportation and communication were two elements needed to combat the effects of the floodwater. Without these items marginally in place, it would be almost impossible to coordinate and transport relief supplies to where they were most needed.

The wire chief and his staff were so overwhelmed with appeals for assistance that the Bell System had to suspend general business in order to give clear wires to those communities calling for aid. At one point, Green received a personal call from his home telling him that his wife was seriously ill. A doctor advised him that that his wife needed to have a surgical operation immediately, and at that moment, Green had to consider what his priority should be. His wife solved his dilemma by asking the doctor to pass on the word that Green should remain at his post because others were giving her the best care possible and he should continue doing the same for others in need.

Elsewhere in the Ohio Valley, the White River at Indianapolis, Indiana, had overrun one-third of that city. Peru, Indiana, was being practically swept off the map by the high waters of the Wabash River. And in the wake of this havoc, Frank Wampler, who was the district commercial manager of the Central Union Telephone Company, was continually at the elbow of Governor Ralston of Indiana night and day. As the person in charge of telephone services, Mr. Wampler spent his time scheming, planning and implementing creative ways of maintaining an open line for heeding and helping the people whom the misfortune of flooding had overwhelmed.

Back in Omaha, Nebraska, at the Webster exchange, the flow of vital information was maintained by Etta Larsen and her switchboard associates with bleeding and bruised hands; the ladies worked with unfailing intensity for forty-eight hours following the Easter Sunday tornados. Many true stories could easily be told about the chronicle of heroic deeds and duties extremely well performed from wind-torn Omaha to half-submerged Marietta, Ohio, and still the full story would fall short of completion.

Wheeling, West Virginia, and Zanesville, Ohio

During the great flood, the banks of the Ohio River made no distinction regarding the state line between Ohio and West Virginia. Across the Ohio River in Wheeling, West Virginia, on Market Street just south of Fourteenth Street, was a pond of muddy water where many interesting and often serious scenes were taking place during the day and nights of the 1913 flood. Boats of almost every description were being paddled or rowed on the streets and in the storerooms and other places of business. Those who were riding past were able to see distinctly and clearly that a significant amount of damage was being heaped on Wheeling. The district between Fifteenth Street and the creek bridge was severely handicapped as a result of the water, and excluding the fact that the water reached far above the first floor of all business establishments in that section, Market Street might have queerly resembled a small Venice, Italy. Parties of every description, and sightseers in particular, plied back and forth on the waters, and although the winds at times were biting and cold, those who were out apparently showed no concern.

The two bridges on the Ohio side of the river and the street fronting on the river, not affected by the water, attracted thousands of sightseers to the waterfront. The high river seems to have had an irresistible charm for many, and hundreds stood about by the hour watching the swift water and debris pass downriver.

Boats were at a premium, and at times, there were dozens of persons standing on the high places and in buildings along the route, awaiting an

Many wood-frame homes were literally picked up by the swiftly flowing floodwater and moved off their stone foundations. *LOC.*

opportunity to secure a boat to go either to the business district or to South Wheeling. Many others, who were returning from their daily work, were held up by the small number of boats. In many cases, exorbitant prices were charged for a trip because given the choice of riding in a boat or swimming, people preferred to part with their coins.

Every aspect of life was affected by the flood, and the list of things that had gone wrong was endless. The flood caught many businessmen on Main Street unprepared, and as a result, the loss would be very heavy for some. Merchandise of every description was caught in the rise, and one local wholesale house reported that practically everything on the first floor had been lost. One saloon on the south side was apparently vacated by the proprietor hurriedly, as much of the inventory stock, including a line of choice liquors, was left on the shelves, affording a temptation to many to try to get inside the establishment. In a restaurant and confectionery on Market Street, sausages and a bunch of bananas were left hanging in the window. Furniture, food and fixtures could be seen floating around on the water within the buildings. Several roadbed washouts along the National Road were reported around Fulton, Glendale and other points as a result of the heavy rains. The Dieringer corner grocery was well under water, and very little of the contents was saved. Steamboat activity was entirely suspended, as it was impossible for any craft of any size to get under the bridges spanning the Ohio with the present prevailing stage of water. The A.D. Mead Company sustained considerable loss by not being able to move the furniture to the second floor. All of Mead's chickens, including the prized Buff Orpingtons and the Leghorns, drowned.

Considerable valuable freight is said to have been caught in the P.C.C. and St. Louis railroad freight station by the rapid rise of the Ohio River and its tributary streams. The water came up so fast that it was impossible to get all of the freight out. Wheeling and Moundsville were completely cut off to travel because washouts along the narrows were causing considerable trouble. Men were reported to have been working on the road all day to get it back in shape. The entire fire department responded to a call for a residential fire that was caused by a gas explosion. The department responded, under orders from Chief Rose, in order to immediately check the potential of any more possible fires due to gas leaks and broken gas lines. Wheeling police chief Hastings had received a long-distance appeal from H. Selkowitch, of the chamber of commerce of Zanesville, Ohio, asking for help. Zanesville was from five to ten feet under water, martial law prevailed and the city's food supply was running short.

Among the great sufferers from the March floods was the city of Zanesville, Ohio, which is located on opposite banks of the Muskingum River. The water rose to the unprecedented height of fifty-three feet. This was sixteen feet above all known or recorded high-water marks. This unusual rise threw currents of intense rushing water through the streets of both the business and residential districts. While only two lives were lost, the percentage of those rendered homeless was greater than in any other city in Ohio except for Hamilton. Zanesville incurred more than 8,000 people left homeless, 1,320 people distressed or injured and 450 houses completely destroyed. Words could not begin to describe the pain and suffering or portray the destruction of property.

Operators Arline Barnell and Lillian Harvey passed the fearful call for help from Zanesville, Ohio, to Pittsburgh. This was because their phone lines were cut off from the capital city of Columbus after the river reached a stage forty feet higher than the previous record. Two young linemen, Mr. C.M. Conaway and Mr. C.C. Cazer, were dispatched from Columbus to go to Zanesville and help reestablish telephone wire service. They had traveled only four miles when the dark of night overtook them and made the road no longer distinguishable. As a result, their automobile became mired in a sea of mud. So, Conaway and Cazer borrowed an electric car that took them

Two telephone linemen, Mr. C.M. Conaway (left) and Mr. C.C. Cazer, literally endured life-threatening perils and high water in order to maintain an open line of communication between Columbus and Zanesville so the governor and other state officials could coordinate rescue and relief efforts. *CML.*

Zanesville residents used boats as common transportation for a number of days following the flood as the Muskingum River water level took more than a week to subside. *CML.*

as far as Hebron, where they spent the night. At daylight the next morning, they secured a truck and started again. This time, they were able to reach a point that was within two miles of Zanesville when they encountered water so deep that they had to abandon the truck. Next, they constructed a raft of heavy timbers and by the force of pushing and paddling were able to get within one mile of their objective.

Landing at Gant Park, they were able to see the terrible havoc that the Muskingum River had heaped on the community. As in other towns, railroad bridges were gone, and they observed houses and barns being carried downstream. The famous Y-bridge was completely submerged. These two highly competent linemen had kept a line open behind them that had a good circuit to Newark. Cazer had secured a magneto telephone from a rural subscriber near the point where they had built the raft. By placing this phone in a house in Gant Park, he established a temporary station, and from this point, company officials and Governor Cox received information and updates.

While Cazer was working at Gant Park, Conaway secured a small boat and, at the risk of his own life, started across the river while battling the fierce current of the Muskingum to get to the business district. The simple crossing was not easy. Conaway narrowly escaped being capsized by a floating railroad boxcar and from being entangled in poles and wires that were floating down the river. He briefly ran aground on a partially submerged railroad bridge that had been torn from its foundations but was finally able to land in the area of Zanesville known as the "Terrace." From there, he pulled the small boat over to the Fifth Street Bridge and again launched the craft into the swift current. Once more, Conaway was continuously menaced by flood wreckage of all kinds until he finally landed near the Central Union telephone exchange. Completely exhausted, this short journey took three hours after leaving his work partner at Gant Park. At the exchange, he ascertained the level of need and damage to the community to date. The next day, after resting, he returned to Gant Park using the same method and encountering similar perils. From the temporary station at Gant Park, the two men relayed the first authentic information back to Columbus regarding the damage sustained at Zanesville. On the basis of this report, plans for relief and the restoration of other services were initiated.

Meanwhile, at the Zanesville telephone exchange building, water had begun entering the basement through the cable conduits. The exchange staff obtained a fire engine pumper from the Weller-Thomas Chemical Company and started pumping out the water as fast as it entered. The staff also finally succeeded in carrying a telephone line across the floodwater and currents flowing over a bridge to reestablish an open line to Columbus. The great loyalty and devotion to duty by all the staff at this exchange helped significantly to reduce the pain and suffering that the flood had laid on the community. In 1913, without question, the telephone proved to be the most indispensable of all utilities.

Chillicothe and Dayton

The early morning of Wednesday, March 26, 1913, has long been remembered in Chillicothe as the time when a huge tsunami-like flood of the Scioto River beyond all records suddenly came crashing across the city. The waters inflicted tremendous damage and in all took the lives of eighteen people locally. Every small stream and tributary in the Scioto Valley left its banks, and the river very quickly rose to an unprecedented height. On Tuesday, March 25, the river was far above all previous flood records in Columbus, and a critical warning that was sent through the Bell Telephone exchange in Columbus was the first heads up to the people of Chillicothe of what was about to come their way. Human nature being what it is, scant heed was paid to the warning because the old pioneer city had experienced floods in the past and had suffered little. But the city was about to have a new experience involving a flood that would roll over the entire community on Wednesday morning in the gray hours of dawn. At 4:00 a.m., a wall of water swept down the already swollen Scioto River. A few messengers hurried along the streets in the eastern and southern sections of the city bearing words of warning, but the warning came too late.

The river rapidly rose higher and higher until it topped its banks and poured a torrent of water through the town. It rose above the high embankment of the Baltimore and Ohio railway across Yoctangee Park. The water quickly filled the park and continued to rise until it poured across the canal, rushing down Walnut, Park and Paint Streets and roaring destructively through Hickory, Ewing, Poplar Streets and other east end thoroughfares. By 8:00

a.m., more than three-fourths of the city was submerged in a muddy-colored sea of water that extended from High Street to Mount Logan. In the eastern and southern parts of the city, the floodwater was twenty feet deep in some places. The water flowed with such speed and swiftness that the vast majority of people were caught totally off guard and unprepared. They had time only to flee for their lives to the second stories or to rooftops, where they had to hold on as best they could. All the while, they were exposed to the cold and were insufficiently clothed to endure the wet rain and sleet that came down with merciless persistence for the rest of the day.

Powerfully swift water flowed through the streets and alleys of Chillicothe. As in the Columbus Franklinton area, wood-frame buildings were overturned or washed away, and brick masonry buildings were undermined at their foundation and came crashing down. Hickory Street especially was a scene of immense destruction. The brick street paving was washed away. The waters then tore a ravine ranging from ten to twenty feet deep. Ewing Street suffered just as much, and much of the entire east end received the same level of disfigurement. Boats were launched early in the morning in an attempt to rescue those in peril. Many heroic deeds were performed, and hundreds owed their lives to a small army of gallant volunteers. One volunteer of note was Silas Pyle, who gave up his life after saving at least thirty-five people.

All day and night, the dangerous rescue work went on, with a number of families not being brought to safety until late Thursday afternoon. Once again, it is impossible to tell of all the narrow escapes and gallant rescues, but one woman, on crutches with a broken leg, saved her children by opening a hole in the ceiling, starting with a hat pin. Then she lifted them into the loft of their small home as water continued to completely fill the room below. Another man and his wife, holding their little daughter, stood on a long fireplace mantelpiece of their one-story home in the cold floodwater for nearly twenty-four hours. Through the long hours of darkness, their child prayed out loud for help.

In one extraordinary situation, an entire family realized that their house was about to collapse due to the swift currents and managed to jump to the roof of the dwelling immediately next door. Then, the house that they jumped onto also started to fall. So, everyone on that house, a total of thirteen, crossed over to a third house. This time, the transfer was accomplished by means of a quickly improvised bridge from one roof to the other. When the third house began to crumble underneath them, they were all able to reach a loft that stood firm until they were finally rescued. Still another Chillicothe family stayed huddled in a little attic while they

An infirm woman is carried to a relief station through floodwater by volunteers. *LOC.*

Flood refugees make camp and share food and water supplies. *LOC.*

witnessed the front part of the house being washed away and the rest of the structure threatening to give way at any moment as it continually swayed with the winds and currents.

Like Chillicothe, most communities located along streams and rivers in the Ohio had previously experienced flooding. In many communities, the flooding had not resulted in casualties or any real serious problems in the past. The most severe flooding of the 1913 calamity occurred along the Great Miami River in southwestern Ohio, and the conditions in and around the Dayton area were particularly challenging. The Great Miami River flooded fourteen square miles of Dayton and the surrounding vicinity, and muddy water flowed in strong, swift currents throughout downtown streets and alleys. In Dayton alone, the flood claimed the lives of 123 people. Once the flood levees began to fail and collapse, the rushing water began rising as high as twenty feet in the downtown district. This was a part of the same flood that was created by a series of three colliding winter storms that hit the Midwest region in March 1913. Within three days, eight to eleven inches of rain fell throughout the Great Miami River watershed. Because most of the ground was frozen, this resulted in runoff of over 90 percent of the storm water, causing the river and its tributaries to begin overflowing very rapidly.

This flood remains the historic flood of record for the watershed region of the Great Miami River, and the amount of water that passed through the river's channel stream during these storms equaled the flow of water over Niagara Falls each month. The breaking of the levees initiated a series of events that further compounded the devastation. In addition, fires broke out across the city because gas lines were ruptured by the strength of the flood currents, and the fire department was unable to address the fires because getting access with equipment was nearly impossible.

The Great Miami River watershed covers nearly 4,000 square miles and 115 miles of channel that flow south into the Ohio River. As previously described, other cities across Ohio experienced flooding from these storms, but not as extensively as the cities of Dayton, Piqua, Troy and Hamilton along the banks of the Great Miami River.

As an early pioneer town, Dayton was established along the Great Miami River at the convergence of its three tributaries, which include the Stillwater River, the Mad River and Wolf Creek. Uniquely, the four rivers converge within one mile along the river channel near the city's central downtown business district. The local Native Americans, who were most likely members of the Shawnee tribe, warned federal surveyor Israel Ludlow

This photograph illustrates the power of the flood currents as they slam against this bridge in Dayton. *LOC.*

about the recurring flooding in the area when he laid out Dayton in 1795 with Northwest Territory governor Arthur St. Clair, Jonathan Dayton and William McMillan. Before the 1913 flood, the Dayton area experienced major floods nearly every decade, with major water flows in 1805, 1828, 1847, 1866 and 1898. Most of downtown Dayton lies in the Great Miami River's natural flood plain. This would give rise to the claim that Dayton's flood was not caused by a natural flood but by a man-made long-range gamble where the balance became due at once.

The following events took place between Friday, March 21, and Wednesday, March 26, in 1913:

- Friday, March 21, 1913. Good Friday and the first day of spring arrived. Daytime temperatures hovered around sixty degrees. The first storm arrived with heavy rain and winds.
- Saturday, March 22, 1913. The Miami Valley area experienced a calm, sunny day until a second storm arrived. Air temperatures dropped into the twenties, resulting in the rain-saturated ground freezing solid.

This scene of rescue boat operations was a common sight throughout the Ohio Valley region. *LOC.*

Train service was halted in many places because of debris that was deposited on the tracks of railroad bridges by high floodwater. *LOC.*

A streetcar tram and a Model T Ford collided together from the force of heavy flood debris. *LOC.*

- Sunday, March 23, 1913, was Easter Sunday and a time for recognizing God's grace. The entire Ohio River Valley area was hit by torrential rains from a third storm. The saturated and frozen countryside was at its limit of water absorption, and 90 percent of the storm water became rain runoff that flowed directly into the Great Miami River and its tributaries.
- Monday, March 24, 1913. Following a full twenty-four hours, precipitation of between eight and eleven inches caused the river to reach a mark of 11.6 feet by 7:00 a.m., which was the high level for the year, and the water continued to rise.
- Tuesday, March 25, 1913. Starting at midnight, the local Dayton police were advised to warn the community that the Herman Street levee was weakening and would soon fail. City officials responded by activating warning horns, bells, sirens and alarms. Gaylord Cummin, the Dayton city engineer, reported to the mayor at 5:30 a.m. that the floodwater was at the top of the levees and was flowing at the unprecedented rate of 100,000 cubic feet per second. Water overflowing the levees began to appear in the city streets at approximately 6:00 a.m. By 8:00 a.m., the levees on the south side of the central business district had collapsed, and floodwater had started to infiltrate the downtown area. The level of the muddy floodwater continued rising until early the next morning.

Above: This rescue boat is delivering victims to a church on Grand Avenue being used as a relief station in Dayton. *LOC*.

Left: The publisher of the *Dayton Daily News*, James Middleton Cox (1870–1957), had only been the Ohio governor for nine weeks when the 1913 statewide flood occurred. *LOC*.

- Wednesday, March 26, 1913. Sometime at about 1:30 a.m. this morning, the floodwater reached a record crest of twenty feet deep in the downtown business district. Later in the morning, at the intersection of Fifth Street and Wilkinson, a ruptured gas line caused an explosion that ignited a fire that wiped out almost an entire city block. Numerous ruptured gas lines were responsible for the fires that took place throughout the city. The fire department again was unable to gain access to these fires because of the high water conditions, and many additional buildings were lost.

As soon as the floodwater began receding, a massive cleanup effort commenced. Governor Cox ordered Ohio National Guard troops into the area to secure order, protect life and property by preventing looting and support the recovery efforts. Throughout the state, the members of the National Guard were unable to reach their assigned posts for several days because of the washed-out roads and the general high water conditions. Once they arrived at their assigned communities, they wasted no time constructing refugee tent camps for families who had been permanently or temporarily displaced from their homes.

During this time, John H. Patterson, a local businessman who founded the National Cash Register Company, took an advanced civic role in championing the recovery efforts. He was closely assisted by his sales manager, Thomas J. Watson. Patterson had his employees construct nearly three hundred flat-bottomed boats and also organized rescue teams to save

National Cash Register Company employees quickly built nearly three hundred flat-bottomed boats to be used to rescue local residents. *LOC.*

Above: Throughout the state following the flood, decomposing bodies were found by volunteers and transported to the morgue. *PC*.

Opposite, top: A temporary morgue was established at NCR campus for the dead victims found in Dayton. *LOC*.

Opposite, bottom: This dog became an orphan after his entire owner family fell victim to high floodwater. *LOC*.

the thousands of people stranded on the roofs and upper stories of buildings. He organized intensive relief efforts throughout the community, even going as far as opening his own factories on Stewart Street to be used as emergency shelters to provide food and lodging for those who had been driven from their homes. Patterson also quickly organized local doctors and nurses to provide urgently needed medical care.

The aftermath of the flood was no means a pleasant sight and stripped much of Dayton of its post–Civil War neighborhood charm and tree-lined thoroughfares. As the water receded, the damages were assessed in the Dayton area as taking the following toll on the general welfare of the community:

- More than 360 people died during the flood, mostly through drowning and exposure to cold weather.
- Nearly 65,000 people were displaced due to their homes collapsing or rendered temporarily uninhabitable due to floodwater and debris.

These horses are struggling to survive the swiftly flowing floodwater in downtown Dayton. *LOC.*

These mules survived the flood only because they were deposited on a residential rooftop during high floodwater. *LOC.*

The Delco plant in Dayton being cleaned following the flood. This facility had manufactured the first electric starter for car. *LOC.*

- About 21,100 homes were completely destroyed, and many were washed downstream.
- Nearly 1,380 horses and 2,150 other domestic animals and pets drowned during the flood.
- Brick paved streets, streetlights and unearthed service utilities were completely washed downstream.
- Buildings were moved off their foundations, and large debris in the water such as trees, railroad components and streetcars caused severe damage to other structures.
- The estimated cost of physical property damage to homes and businesses, including factories and railroads, was more than $100 million (or more than $2 billion in today's dollar value).

The cleanup, repair and reconstruction efforts took about one year following the flood damage. The general economic impact of the flood took the better part of a decade to overcome. Much of this was due to the supply production during World War I that greatly fueled the local economy. Unfortunately, the destruction from the flood was the leading cause of the scarcity of old and historical architectural landmarks and buildings in the central core of downtown Dayton.

A Plan of Solutions and Opposition to Common Sense

Instead of accepting flooding as an inevitable recurring nightmare, the people of the Dayton-area community were determined to prevent a future disaster of this magnitude. Bolstered by John Patterson's personal determination to develop a controlled watershed district, on March 27, 1913, Governor Cox appointed members of the Dayton Citizens Relief Commission. In the wake of this tragedy, Miami Valley citizens rallied to initiate plans to prevent future flooding, and in May, the commission sponsored a ten-day fundraiser. Some twenty-three thousand citizens contributed more than $2 million to begin a comprehensive flood protection program on a valley-wide basis. With these funds, the commission acquired the service of hydrological engineer Arthur Morgan to come up with an extensive plan for a capital improvement project to protect the Dayton area from future flooding. The result was a state-of-the-art flood protection system made up of five concrete dams consisting of the Huffman, Germantown, Englewood, Lockington and Taylorsville facilities and a series of levees that has successfully protected the Miami Valley from flooding by the Great Miami River since 1922.

As the project administrator, Morgan secured the services of nearly fifty consulting engineers to analyze the Miami Valley watershed, historic climate and precipitation patterns, as well as to determine water volume potential of future floods. They even analyzed global flood data for information about general flooding patterns throughout the world. Based on this analysis, five months later, Morgan presented eight different flood control plans to the

City of Dayton and local county officials. In the end, the officials endorsed and selected a plan based on the flood control system in the Loire Valley in France. The design of this particular system would consist of five earthen dams and extensive modifications to the various river channels that converge and flow through Dayton. The dams would be equipped with conduits and flumes to release a limited amount of water as needed. The wider river channels would be buffered by levees supported by a series of smaller secondary levees. In addition, flood storage areas behind the dams would be used for agricultural production between the times of flooding. Morgan's goal was to develop a flood plan that would handle 140 percent of the water capacity experienced during the 1913 flood. The analysis had calculated the boundaries of the river channel in the event of a one-thousand-year major flood. In addition, it was highly recommended that all commerce located in the flood plain area should be relocated.

With the plan supported by Governor Cox, Dayton attorney John McMahon worked on drafting the Vonderheide Act, better known as the Ohio Conservancy Law. The Ohio legislature passed the act in 1914. It was this law that allowed local governments to begin defining conservancy districts for the purpose of regional flood control. Controversial elements of the act gave local governments the right to raise money for the civil engineering services through taxes and the power to use eminent domain to support the purchase or condemnation of the necessary lands for flood plains, dams and basins. In 1915, as a result of the Vonderheide Act, the Miami Conservancy District was created, with Arthur Morgan appointed the first president. As another Ohio original, this became the first major watershed district in the United States.

The constitutionality of the Vonderheide Act was challenged by a lawsuit brought by a landowner affected by eminent domain in *Orr v. Allen*, and attempts were made to amend it through the Garver-Quinlisk Bills. The legal battle continued from 1915 to 1919 and was heard in both the Ohio and United States Supreme Court. In the end, the law was upheld.

Since its origin, the Miami Conservancy District has saved the region from flooding more than 1,500 times over the decades. Operational expenses for maintaining the district come from an annual property tax assessment collected from all property owners in the district. Properties in proximity to the river channels and the natural flood plain are assessed at a higher rate than properties that are farther away.

An interesting outcome of the flood control program had to do with a small village named Osborn, Ohio, which was the community most affected by the aftermath of the flood. It should be noted that Osborn received very little damage from the flood, and the village was located squarely in the area specified to become part of the new Huffman flood plain. The main railroad lines of the New York Central, the Erie and the Ohio Electric Railway tracks that ran through Osborn were relocated several miles south to run through the community of Fairfield, Ohio.

In 1921, with the financial backing of the Miami Conservancy District, the residents of Osborn chose to move their houses instead of abandoning the structures, and almost four hundred houses were carefully moved three miles to new foundations along Hebble Creek adjacent to Fairfield. In 1949, the two towns voted to merge into one municipality. The name of the new town was changed in 1950 to Fairborn, Ohio, in order to reflect the merging of the two communities.

There were many architectural landmarks and personal items lost during the flood, but Ohio's history of flight heritage also suffered a great loss. Dayton, Ohio, was the home of the brothers Orville and Wilbur Wright, who were the first to sustain flight with a powered, controlled aircraft a decade before the flood. After their historic 1903 flight, they focused their attention on creating the new aviation industry, designing and building in their workshop and testing the aircraft in a field around Huffman Prairie, which was located adjacent to the newly planned Huffman Dam. The Wright brothers made it a point to meticulously document their test flights using a camera and had an extensive collection of glass photographic plates. One unfortunate loss from the flood was water damage, which created cracks and blemishes on the glass photographic plates. The photograph prints made from the plates before the flood were of higher quality than the prints made after the flood. However, very few prints were developed off the glass negatives before 1913. This was because the Wrights kept the records and any proof of their ingenious pioneering work a secret from the public because of issues relating to patent infringements. A good number of these plates were lost. Some survived but provided only marginal-quality photos. Sadly, many irreplaceable images of great historic moments of early flight were lost.

Arthur Ernest Morgan (1878–1975) was a civil engineer and an educator. He was also the design engineer and project construction administrator for the Miami Conservancy District flood control system. He later served as the president of Antioch College between 1920 and 1936. He was also the first chairman of Tennessee Valley Authority from 1933 until 1938, during which he implemented the proven concepts from his earlier collaboration with the

Miami Conservancy District. Morgan was born in Ohio, but his family soon relocated to a small town in Minnesota. Following high school graduation, he worked as a laborer and assistant to several surveyors in Colorado. During this time, he learned that in America there was a deficiency of the practical understanding of hydraulic engineering principles. This conclusion is backed up by pioneer surveyor Israel Ludlow paying little heed to the warnings of the Native Americans regarding recurring floods in the Miami Valley area. Once Morgan returned home, he became a civil engineering apprentice under his father's supervision and began learning the practical applications of hydraulic engineering. By 1910, he had established his own engineering firm and was closely affiliated with the American Society of Civil Engineers.

Hydrological engineer Arthur Morgan was the engineer who proposed and supervised the flood control projects for the Miami Conservancy District. *LOC.*

After the great Dayton, Ohio flood in 1913, local civic leaders selected Arthur Morgan to be the project manager for a new concept of flood control. As a practical and experienced hydraulic engineer, Morgan proposed an intricate system of dry earthen dams and concrete levees to control the Miami Valley watershed drainage north of Dayton. Before implementation, his design concepts were challenged all the way to the U.S. Supreme Court. Of the many reasons given for the opposition, one of the weakest had to do with his lack of a college education and formal engineering training. The Supreme Court eventually ruled in favor of Morgan's plan, and construction began. Upon completion of this massive project, and in subsequent years, the effectiveness of his concepts has prevented the recurrence of large-scale flooding in the Dayton metropolitan area time and time again. Because of this success, he was selected in 1933 to design, build and implement the Tennessee Valley Authority system of dams to integrate natural resource management for flood control, electric power production, navigation, malaria prevention, reforestation and erosion control.

John Henry Patterson (1844–1922) was regarded highly by nearly the entire Dayton community for his unselfish giving and support of the unfortunate victims of the flood. He was an industrialist and founder of the National Cash Register Company (NCR). He was a businessperson and salesperson. He also coined a phrase for his service division: "We Cannot Afford to Have a Single Dissatisfied Customer." Many prominent corporate businessmen received their training at Patterson's sales training school called Sugar Camp on the grounds of the NCR factory campus in Dayton. Following Dayton's Great Flood of 1913, Patterson worked in collaboration with state and local governments to implement his vision of a managed watershed for the Great Miami River district. His efforts resulted in the development of the Miami Conservancy District, which is regarded as one of the first major flood control districts in America. The Great Flood also resulted in John Patterson and his assistant, Thomas Watson, being forgiven after being convicted in a federal antitrust lawsuit.

Thomas John Watson Sr. (1874–1956) was John Patterson's right hand in organizing and facilitating the outstanding relief efforts and humanitarian deeds on behalf of the National Cash Register Company in Dayton following the flood. It is interesting that Patterson was renowned for having hired and subsequently fired Watson, who went on to become general manager, then president, of Computing Tabulating Recording Company (CTR), later renamed International Business Machines Corporation (IBM). As the chairman and CEO of IBM, Watson stirred the company's growth into an international conglomerate from 1914 to 1956. Using much of what he learned at NCR, Watson developed IBM's renowned corporate management style and culture. At the time of his death in 1956, Watson was one of the wealthiest self-made industrialists of his time and was regarded as the world's greatest salesman.

The years before the Dayton flood in 1913, Watson, under Patterson's direction, set a goal to completely eliminate any competition in the used cash register market. With the financial backing of NCR, he established a completely independent organization known as the Watson Cash Register and Second Hand Exchange in New York City. By grossly undercutting the competition on behalf of NCR, he gradually monopolized the business until he was able to buy out his competitors. He then moved to Philadelphia and, after that, progressed across the country, repeating the operation and covertly establishing another near monopoly for NCR, in the secondhand business,

John H. Patterson (1844–1922) led the recovery efforts. Patterson organized rescue teams to save the thousands of people stranded on roofs and the upper stories of buildings. He turned the NCR factory on Stewart Street into an emergency shelter, providing food and lodging, and he organized local doctors and nurses to provide medical care. *LOC.*

NCR's Thomas J. Watson Sr. worked closely with John Patterson to give prompt aid to the flood victims and refugees of Dayton. Watson later became the chairman and CEO of IBM. *LOC.*

to match that already established in the new machine market. In 1908, the secondhand cash register business was merged into NCR's sales operation, and Watson was appointed assistant sales manager. He subsequently became the sales manager in 1910. In addition, he also worked with the NCR engineering staff in developing new products with advanced technology.

The methods Watson used to achieve success in the secondhand cash register market were viewed by many as a clear and blatant disregard for federal antitrust laws. Consequently, on February 22, 1912, John Patterson and Thomas Watson, along with more than two dozen other NCR managers and executives, were indicted for being in breach of federal antitrust laws. Upon the completion of the litigation on February 13, 1913, Watson was found guilty and sentenced to a $5,000 fine plus one year in Miami County jail. The sentence requiring time to be spent in jail caught Watson by surprise because generally only a monetary fine was imposed in such cases. During the time that Watson was appealing the judgment, the charges against Patterson were promptly dismissed because of his philanthropic and humanitarian efforts during the Dayton flood disaster of 1913. In due time and probably because of his contribution to the Dayton flood relief program, Watson won his appeal, which meant that the verdict was postponed pending a new trial. President Woodrow Wilson later issued a pardon for both Patterson and Watson because of their leadership roles in dealing with the aftermath of Great Dayton Flood.

A long political battle followed the passing of the Vonderheide Conservancy Act. Farmers in the counties to the north of Dayton, whose rich agricultural lands were to be flooded by the dams, vigorously opposed the plan. They challenged the constitutionality of the act in the courts and attempted to amend it with the Garver-Quinlisk Bills. Their opposition to the flood control plan was unwisely based on the following weak issues and falsehoods:

- The law illegally established a political subdivision with a board of directors that was given the power to tax and to move existing transportation systems such as railroads, bridges and roads.
- The Vonderheide Act significantly underestimated the monetary costs and amount of land needed (thirty-eight thousand acres as opposed to the opposition's estimate of seventy thousand acres).
- The dam and reservoir system was not a feasible solution for the Mad River and Miami Valley.
- The dams and reservoirs would flood cities such as Tippecanoe City, Troy, DeGraff, Lewistown, Lake View, Osborn, Medway, Tremont and Bowlusville, which normally would not have been subject to flooding.

OBSTRUCTING THE WAY

This cartoon depicted the issue of flood control as the top public concern after the flood. The public was not interested in any opposition or political games from state legislators. *WSUL.*

- The prior practice in Ohio had been to drain flooded land as quickly as possible, but the Vonderheide Act specified holding the water as a supply resource in reservoirs.
- The Vonderheide Act called for everyone to pay taxes that would be used to benefit all the communities in the conservancy district; however, those opposed to the act argued that their tax dollars should only go to pay for efforts in their own community.

In 1915, *Reasons Why the Garver-Quinlisk Bill Should Be Enacted*, a book published and distributed by the opposition to the Conservancy Law, the dissenters stated the following:

> *The Dayton people exhibited no picture of any work on their part by way of cleaning out the channel or removing obstruction; neither did they show, nor can*

they show, any picture of a Detention Reservoir used to back up water on fertile lands for protection of their land, and while we do not wish to intimate that our neighbors in the city of Dayton, by enactment of the above prevision, or by authority conferred by said section, hope to reap some benefit from the erection of dams and reservoirs in the Miami and Mad River Valleys, by the utilization of the water for power in their municipalities, and at the expense of the property owner about said dams, and included in any such district, yet such is possible, for by the provision of said Act they would clearly have the right to utilize said water, so impounded, for purposes other than protection against flood.

It was further stated that "the Act, as it stands, should be entitled, An Act to prevent floods in one part of the country by producing floods in another part and, in order to accomplish this, to deprive the people of the locality of all voice in the matter."

An End to Menacing Opposition: The Final Decision

In June 1915, after two years of litigation and legal stalling, the Supreme Court of Ohio ruled to sustain the Vonderheide Conservancy Act in its entirety. The Supreme Court's decision included upholding the right of the Conservancy District to levy taxes, one of the major issues of debate. The court named E.A. Deeds of Dayton, Gordon Rentschler of Hamilton and Henry M. Allen of Troy as directors of the Conservancy District.

U.S. Supreme Court; ORR V. ALLEN, *Submitted October 14, 1918, Decided December 9, 1918*

Appeal from the District Court of the United States for the Southern District of Ohio

Syllabus: The "Conservancy Act of Ohio," designed to prevent floods and authorizing creation of drainage districts and drainage improvements through administrative boards empowered to exert eminent domain, and to tax, assess for benefits, and issue bonds, affords full opportunity for testing private grievances judicially, and, as correctly construed by the court below, is consistent with the state and federal constitutions.

Above: John Patterson and Edward Deeds contributed to the rebuilding of Dayton, and their vision for a managed watershed for the Great Miami River resulted in the development of the Miami Conservancy District after the Great Flood of 1913. *CML*.

Left: U.S. Supreme Court justice Edward White upheld the Ohio Vonderheide Act, which established flood control conservancy districts throughout the state. *LOC*.

The case was stated in the memorandum opinion by the Chief Justice Edward Douglass White [White was nominated to be the 9th Chief Justice of the U.S. Supreme court by President William Howard Taft of Ohio].

The "Conservancy Act of Ohio" is the name given the statute by its first section. Its seventy-nine sections are thus epitomized in the title: "To prevent floods, to protect cities, villages, farms, and highways from inundation, and to authorize the organization of drainage and conservation districts."

The Ohio General Code, 6828-1 to 6828-79; Laws of Ohio, vol. 104, p. 13. The statute was admittedly designed to prevent the recurrence of the unprecedented and disastrous flood which invaded the Miami Valley in 1913. Briefly, there was provision for drainage districts, for boards to plan, construct, and maintain the works contemplated, with the right to exert eminent domain, and to raise money by taxation, by assessments for benefits, and, in some cases, by issue of bonds. Every person affected who was aggrieved was undoubtedly given ample means by the statute to test judicially his grievance. A district was organized embracing land along each side of the Miami River which had been flooded in 1913 or which was required for reservoir sites or for furnishing material.

The appellant was a citizen of California owning property within this district who filed his bill to prohibit the enforcement of the statute on the ground that it was repugnant to both the constitution of the state and that of the United States.

In short summary, the final judgment and the past one hundred years of first-rate performance of Ohio's flood control infrastructure have proved to have been the right decision and plan. This history demonstrates that the opponents to the Conservancy Act of Ohio were lacking in enthusiasm for civic responsibility and in many ways not able to embrace the new challenge of urban life in the twentieth century. It was obvious that during the flood the opponents never had to recall making a promise in the attic that their family would never again have to endure such a horrifying experience.

Epilogue

The Test of Readiness and Lessons Learned

The test of readiness and whether lessons were learned continues every year during the autumn and spring flood seasons. The years 1937 and 1959 were flood events marginally similar in circumstances to the 1913 flood. Furthermore, it is generally felt that the flood control improvements that followed the 1913 flood proved to be wise actions injected into strategic long-range planning that continues to secure and protect the communities that they serve. For many people who were twenty years old or younger during the March 1913 flood, they also witnessed the 1937 and 1959 high-water events.

During the Great Depression era between January 13 and 25, 1937, six to twelve inches of rain fell over Ohio. Such a volume of precipitation had never been experienced prior or since over such a large region of Ohio. January 1937 remains as the highest precipitation month ever recorded for Ohio.

The 1937 flood drastically affected the Cincinnati area from January 18 to February 5 by leaving one hundred thousand people homeless. The Ohio River initially began to rise because of a large volume of rainfall in the West Virginia and Pennsylvania hills. The river reached its peak on January 26, at 79.9 feet, and the water levels on January 26 and 27 were the highest ever recorded from Gallipolis downstream past Cincinnati toward the Indiana state line. The water crests were 20.0 to 28.0 feet in some places above the normal flood stage and 4.0 to 9.0 feet above the previous record set during the 1884 flood. About 10 percent of the city's area was flooded, and streetcar transportation service was curtailed. Cincinnati's drinking water supply and main pumping station were crippled. Among the flooded structures was Crosley Field, home field of the Cincinnati Reds baseball team. Additionally, the amusement park Coney Island was submerged, and the sculptured wooden carousel horses were washed downstream. Some of horses were finally recovered downriver near Paducah, Kentucky.

At Portsmouth, the rising river threatened to top the flood wall that was built to extend ten feet above the normal flood stage. In order to prevent a catastrophic breach of the flood wall, like with the levee in Columbus during the 1913 flood, city engineers and officials intentionally opened the floodgates to permit river water to flood the business district eight to ten feet deep.

As a result of the flood control measures instituted by the Ohio Conservancy Act, the Columbus and Dayton areas suffered no real ill effects from the January 1937 torrential rains. Statewide, only 10 people died in contrast to more than 460 killed in the floods of March 1913.

STATEWIDE FLOODING: JANUARY 21, 1959

In January 1959, after three to six inches of rain fell on the frozen winter ground of Ohio, flood conditions similar to the March 1913 catastrophe revisited the region. The streets of Mansfield were under four feet of water, and industries were closed by floodwater in Youngstown and Canton. Columbus was the most severely affected of Ohio's major cities, with many streets flooded, one hundred homes badly damaged and 3,200 evacuees cared for at Red Cross shelters. Much of Columbus' flood problem in 1959 could have been alleviated with an adequate flood wall around the Franklinton area—one was finally erected in 2004. One-third of Chillicothe was flooded when the Scioto River broke through a levee of sandbags. High water and ice jams on the Sandusky River caused flooding in Upper Sandusky, Tiffin and Fremont. Deaths and devastation were considerably less than in the 1913 flood because the 1959 flood was made less intense by the flood control dams and reservoirs that were constructed after 1913. Also, general communication and advance warning systems were more efficient. This resulted in the rescue work being better organized and made more effective, with better structurally reinforced bridges and building foundations.

CLEVELAND'S GREAT LAKES HURRICANE: NOVEMBER 9–11, 1913

Some meteorologists believe that this unusual hurricane event was also a result of the volcanic winter that resulted following the June 1912 eruption of the Novarupta and Katmai Volcanoes.

Severe weather events continued well into the autumn of 1913. An immense storm that ravaged the Great Lakes in November 1913 has historically been referred to as the "Big Blow," the "Freshwater Fury" and the "Great Lakes Hurricane." It was a blizzard with hurricane-force winds that devastated the Great Lakes Basin in the Midwest and the Canadian province of Ontario from November 7 to November 10, 1913. Generally, storms of such magnitude and with such high wind velocities do not last more than four or five hours. But this raging Great Lakes storm continued for more than sixteen hours, with an average speed of sixty miles per hour and frequent bursts of more than seventy-five miles per hour. It crippled ship traffic on the lakes and throughout the Great Lakes region and was one of the most severe winter storms in Cleveland's history.

In a similar fashion as the March flood weather conditions, the November 1913 storm began with the convergence of two major storm fronts. The two weather fronts were quickly fueled by the warm waters of the Great Lakes. This is a seasonal process or convergence that is commonly referred to as a "November gale" or "November witch," and it is this condition that produces lake effect snow from the late fall through the winter. This precipitation condition is the result of a cold blast of air passing over warm water. These cold blasts originate in the polar regions of Canada and pass over the water of the Great Lakes, and this causes warmer air and moisture to form. The warm air rises above the cold air and creates the snow and cloudy visibility conditions know as whiteouts. This occurs on the downwind side of the shorelines, which, in this case is Ohio's Lake Erie shore, where Cleveland is located. In November 1913, it produced ninety-mile-per-hour winds, waves more than thirty-five feet high and whiteout snow squalls.

Many of the same conditions that crippled communications and caused havoc during the March storms also plagued the Cleveland area in November. Freezing rain and wet snow coated telegraph, telephone and electric wires within hours of the storm starting. This was made worse as winds more than fifty miles per hour began toppling power and communication lines, poles and trees. At one point, the average wind speed hitting Cleveland was recorded at seventy-nine miles per hour. Snow and sleet precipitation

Flood currents washing a bridge away in Cleveland during the November 1913 Great Lakes Storm and resulting flood. *LOC.*

Cleveland volunteers were used to remove snow from around fire hydrants and streetcar intersections as a result of the November 1913 blizzard. *LOC.*

fell for two days and accounted for more than twenty-two inches of snow covering Cleveland. Most of eastern Ohio recorded snowfall ranging from eighteen to twenty-five inches. The roofs of several large buildings in Cleveland collapsed because of the increased weight of snow loads. The City of Cleveland service department had to mobilize more than three hundred men and fifty teams of horses to remove the snow from clogged street intersections to allow streetcars to pass.

Due to the desperate need to heat homes and buildings, there was fear of a fire disaster in Cleveland because it was difficult to move and transport firefighting equipment through the heavy snow. Public volunteers were asked to clear three to four feet of drifted snow from around fire hydrants. In some cases, the team of horses required to pull a coal-fired pumping engine had to be increased from three to five horses. The additional seventeen inches of snow that were dumped on Cleveland filled the streets with snowdrifts six feet high. Streetcar operators lived in their marooned vehicles for two nights and ate whatever food was shared by local residents or shopkeepers, who were also stranded. Travelers were forced to take shelter and wait for things to clear. The drifting snow and ice impeded the mobility of trains on railroad lines and trucks on streets, causing a shortage of food and milk to develop. Some rural farmers transported milk from dairies on horse-drawn sleds, and many families had to walk through high snow to a dairy for milk, cheese and butter.

The storm was most powerful on Sunday, November 9, battering and overturning ships on four of the five Great Lakes, particularly Lake Huron. All shipping was halted on Monday, November 10, and part of Tuesday along the St. Lawrence River around Montreal, Quebec. The deceptive lulls in the storm and the lack of prompt and accurate weather reports contributed immensely to the storm's devastation. The most destructive natural disaster ever to hit the Great Lakes destroyed nineteen ships and stranded nineteen others, as well as caused the loss of cargo totaling about 68,300 tons of grain and materials such as coal and iron ore. Of the nineteen ships destroyed, twelve were commercial cargo ships that were lost with their entire crews, consisting of at least 235 sailors. An additional 3 victims from the cargo ship *William Nottingham* were also lost after they had volunteered to leave the ship on a lifeboat in search of help. As the lifeboat was being lowered into the water, a huge wave slammed it into the side of the freighter. The wave knocked all three men into the near-freezing water, where they quickly disappeared.

This public streetcar was marooned in the 1913 Cleveland blizzard. The conductor spent several days living in the streetcar and was provided food by local residents. *LOC.*

The capsized hull of the bulk freighter SS *Charles S. Price* after the November 1913 Great Lakes storm. The entire crew of twenty-eight men lost their lives while transporting iron ore. *LOC.*

Several ship captains recalled that, in some cases, the waves reached about thirty-five feet in height. Being shorter in length than waves ordinarily formed by gales, they occurred in rapid succession, with three waves frequently striking quickly one after another. The captains also observed that the wind often blew in a direction opposite to the waves below. This was due to the storm's cyclonic motion and was a phenomenon that rarely occurs on the Great Lakes.

On Monday, November 10, a capsized vessel was sighted floating on the eastern coast of Michigan near Huronia Beach at the mouth of the St. Clair River. Determining the identity of the vessel became of regional interest and was followed by numerous front-page newspaper articles, but the ship eventually sank after a few days. Six days after it was originally sighted, the ship was identified as the *Charles S. Price*. A crew member named Milton Smith survived only because he acted on a foreboding premonition of doom and chose not to join the *Price* crew at the last moment. He later helped identify the bodies of sailors from the ship that were recovered after being washed ashore.

The following is a list of vessels that sank with no survivors on Lakes Erie, Michigan, Huron and Superior during the 1913 Great Lakes Storm:

- *Plymouth*: seven lives lost
- *Argus*: twenty-eight lives lost
- *James Carruthers*: twenty-two lives lost
- *Hydrus*: twenty-five lives lost
- *John A. McGean*: twenty-eight lives lost
- *Charles S. Price*: twenty-eight lives lost
- *Regina*: twenty lives lost
- *Isaac M. Scott*: twenty-eight lives lost
- *Wexford*: twenty lives lost
- *Buffalo* (lightship): six lives lost
- *Leafield*: eighteen lives lost
- *Henry B. Smith*: twenty-five lives lost

Two ships of interest that were sunk during the 1913 Great Lakes Storm were the SS *James Carruthers*, which was a new ship that had been lunched the same year, and the SS *Henry B. Smith*, which had been launched in 1906.

On Thursday evening, November 6, 1913, the *James Carruthers* completed loading a total of 375,000 bushels of wheat at Fort William, Ontario. Its destination was Midland, Ontario, on the shores of Georgian Bay. The ship's captain, William H. Wright, conferred with another captain, S.A. Lyons of the *J.H. Sheadle*, and both planned to travel down Lake Superior simultaneously. The first hints of the storm began blowing over Lake Superior at about 3:00 a.m. on Saturday, November 8, and the winds quickly shifted from southwest to northwest, bringing with them freezing temperatures, snow squalls and high waves. The *Carruthers* and the *Sheadle* were better than halfway to the Soo Locks when the storm hit.

That evening, both vessels went through the locks and started making their way down the St. Mary's River. On Sunday, November 9, the *Carruthers* was docked at the Picklands, Mather & Company near De Tour, Michigan, to take on a load of coal for fuel. Upon refueling, the Carruthers entered Lake Huron, with the *Sheadle* following a short distance behind. Crew members of the *Sheadle* recalled seeing the lights of the *Carruthers* for a short time as both ships proceeded on a southeastern heading. A little after dawn, the *Carruthers* turned to port on a course that would take it in a straight line to Georgian Bay. This was the last time the *James Carruthers* was ever seen.

Once the great storm subsided on Monday, November 10, a substantial amount of debris and wreckage from a number of different ships started washing up on the shore of Lake Huron. A large field of debris from the *Carruthers* was discovered offshore between Goderich and Kincardine. This location was some seventy miles south of the *Carruthers*'s original course. Several bodies of crew members were also washed ashore near Point Clark. A body with a distinctive red mustache was identified as Captain William Wright. It was evident that the crew had time to prepare for the disaster because the majority of the bodies wore heavy coats and life jackets. Several witnesses living near the shore of Inverhuron, Ontario, heard steamer whistles and sighted distress rockets from a distance during the height of the storm late Sunday afternoon. It was concluded that the rockets were from the *Carruthers* because the bulk of its debris and crew were discovered in this vicinity. Exactly how the brand-new freighter sank and how it came to be so far off course after being bound for Georgian Bay remain mysteries, and the wreck of the SS *James Carruthers* has yet to be located.

The SS *Henry B. Smith* foundered and was lost on November 10, 1913, in Lake Superior during the Great Lakes Storm of 1913 near Marquette, Michigan. It was carrying a load of iron ore at the time of its sinking. The vessel was a steel-hulled, propeller-driven lake freighter built in 1906 by the American Ship Building Company at Lorain, Ohio. The ship was 525 feet in length, 55 feet in width and 31 feet in height, with a gross tonnage of 6,631 and a net tonnage of 5,229. The ship was powered by a triple-expansion steam engine.

Before beginning its last voyage, the *Smith* arrived at Marquette on November 6 to take on a load of iron ore. Over the next two days, a southwest gale swept over Lake Superior, dropping the temperature to twenty-four degrees Fahrenheit. The cold weather caused the damp iron ore to freeze inside the rail hopper cars, and this required a crew of men to climb into the rail car and use a pick and shovel to loosen the ore. This took some time and caused a loading delay for the ship. The *Smith*'s captain, James Owen, had been hounded repeatedly that year by circumstantial delays that resulted in the *Smith* arriving late at various destinations. Consequently, Owen was under considerable pressure because it had been rumored that the ship's owners had made it clear that he had to meet the scheduled delivery deadline or face being dismissed.

On November 9 at about 5:00 p.m., the *Smith* finished loading the iron ore, and since the gale appeared to be in a brief lull, Captain Owen gave orders for the freight vessel to depart. Within minutes after the *Smith* began leaving Marquette Harbor, the fierce winds picked up again, and the storm's lull ended. Witnesses on shore recalled that the *Smith*'s crew desperately tried to close and secure all open hatches. The freighter had a total of thirty-two hatches, and each one needed a crew member's individual attention, with locking bars, clamps and tackle. Even for this experienced crew, securing all the hatches would have required at least two hours of skilled labor. Reacting to the threat of being dismissed, Captain James Owen was now making decisions that compromised the lives of the crew and the ship as the *Henry B. Smith* proceeded directly into one of the worse storms in history with unsecured hatches.

Within twenty minutes of its departure, the full force of the gale struck the *Smith*, with huge waves crashing over the deck, drenching the helpless members of the crew who were struggling in an attempt to close the hatches. Instead of turning to starboard (right) on the usual course for the Soo Locks, Captain Owen ordered the ship turned to port (left), and in doing so, the ship rolled through the high waves as if to capsize. Witnesses to this event on shore concluded that Owen had realized his error and was heading for shelter behind Keweenaw Point to the north. With the encroaching darkness and thick snow squalls, the *Smith* was then lost from sight and never seen again.

Two days following the storm, local residents at the beaches along Shot Point, Chocolay Bay and Laughing Fish Point discovered debris from the *Smith* that had washed up on shore. The wreckage was found high up on the beach, indicating that it had come ashore at the height of the storm. Several days later, the dead body of the ship's second cook, H.R. Haskin,

Above: The bulk freighter SS *Henry B. Smith* and its entire crew of twenty-five were lost during the November 1913 Great Lakes storm and blizzard. *PC*.

Left: Some crew members' bodies from the foundered SS *Wexford* washed ashore near Goderich, Ontario, after the November 1913 Great Lakes Storm. *LOC*.

was found floating about fifty miles west of Whitefish Point. The only other body of the *Smith*'s crew that was later recovered was the skeletal remains of third engineer John Gallagher, found on Parisian Island in the spring of 1914. To date, the wreck of the *Henry B. Smith* has not been located, but it is thought to have probably sunk in deep water some twenty to thirty miles north of Marquette.

Of the twelve ships that sank in the storm, five have never been found. In addition to the *Henry B. Smith* and the *James Carruthers*, the whereabouts of the SS *Leafield*, the SS *Plymouth* and the SS *Hydrus* are unknown. The *Hydrus*, an iron ore freighter, was also following the *Carruthers* on Lake Huron. The wreckage of the SS *Wexford* had been lost for more than eighty-six years until it was discovered in the summer of 2000.

By taking a closer look at the 1913 Great Lakes Storm and its general impact on people, construction engineering and the landscape, it became clear that there was a serious need to modify some critical services and implement improved preparedness. Immediately following the blizzard, Cleveland, Ohio, began a five-year project to relocate all utility cables underground, in conduits beneath major streets.

The loss of so many marine vessels and lives brought heavy criticism of the shipping industry and the shipbuilders. This led to a series of conferences with the insurance and maritime industries to focus on safer designs for shipping vessels. This resulted in the construction of ships with increased stability and longitudinal strength and greater structural integrity.

Another long-term consequence of the Great Lakes Storm followed the complaints filed against the United States Department of Agriculture Weather Bureau offices about alleged unpreparedness. This resulted in increased efforts to achieve more accurate weather forecasting, with quicker comprehension of conditions and communication of proper storm warnings.

Appendix

Significant Events that Shaped the World of 1912–1913

The Great Flood of 1913 was a century ago, and for many today, it is difficult to see any connection to that time or era. But let us not forget that who we are, in many ways, was determined by the events and people of previous times. The baby boomers, their parents and beyond were born and raised with a quality of life closely associated with the aftermath of the Great Flood. Especially in the Miami Valley, these generations were not menaced by floods because of the flood control measures that were implemented in spite of selfish opposition. Floods still occur, as the events are nature's eternal way. Time has demonstrated that what threatens a community can serve to eventually make it stronger by allowing it to become aware of its vulnerabilities. The story of the Great Flood shows us that the severe weather came about following a series of events that began the previous year.

History can be appreciated more fully if we have an understanding of and immerse ourselves into the world as it was during the time being examined. In this way, we are able to make cognitive connections with the past, present and future. An example of this is that in 1913, the baton in the race for equality was inadvertently passed from a former conductor of the Underground Railroad to a person who would help ignite the twentieth-century civil rights movement. Although 1913 was the year Harriet Tubman passed away, Rosa Parks was born five weeks later. The America of this time was the backdrop stage where many of our twentieth-century movers and shakers were born or were in their early developmental childhood. Life was hard, and based on what this new generation witnessed early in life, they proceeded with a determination to make life better in general. The following is a brief overview of significant events, births and a few deaths that occurred during the two years (1912 and 1913) in which events contributing to the flood unfolded.

1912 EVENTS

January 1—The Republic of China is shaped.

January 4—The Scout Association is incorporated throughout the British Commonwealth by Royal Charter.

January 6—New Mexico becomes the forty-seventh state of the United States.

January 17—British polar explorer Captain Robert Falcon Scott and a team of four become the second expeditionary group to reach the South Pole.

February 12—The Qing Dynasty of China, also called the Manchu Dynasty, comes to an end after 268 years.

February 14—Arizona becomes the forty-eighth state and the last of the contiguous states.

March 12—The Girl Scouts of the United States is founded in Savannah, Georgia, by Juliette Gordon Low.

March 17—The Camp Fire Girls is founded by Mrs. Luther Halsey Gulick.

March 23—The Dixie Cup is invented.

March 27—Mayor Yukio Ozaki of Tokyo gives three thousand cherry trees to be planted in Washington, D.C.

March 29—The remaining members of Robert Falcon Scott's South Pole expedition die.

April 10—The RMS *Titanic* departs from Southampton.

April 14—The RMS *Titanic* strikes an iceberg in the northern Atlantic Ocean and sinks, with 1,517 lives lost.

April 16—Harriet Quimby becomes the first woman to fly across the English Channel.

April 20—Fenway Park in Boston, Massachusetts, opens.

April 30—Carl Laemmle founds the Universal Pictures motion picture studio.

May 13—In the United Kingdom, the Royal Flying Corps (forerunner of the Royal Air Force) is established.

June 6—The Novarupta Volcano eruption is the largest in the twentieth century and causes a volcanic winter that contributes to the Great Flood of 1913.

August 27—Edgar Rice Burroughs publishes the literary classic *Tarzan of the Apes.*

September 21—Houdini performs the "Chinese Water Torture Cell" illusion.

September 23—Max Sennett presents the first "Keystone Kops" short film titled *Cohen Collects a Debt.*

September 28—William Christopher Handy introduces an African American folk tradition known as the "blues."

October 14—During an assassination attempt, "Bull Moose" Teddy Roosevelt is shot while campaigning in Milwaukee.

October 17—The Minneapolis Vigilance Committee is formed and, in 1916, changes its name to the Better Business Bureau.

November 5—Arizona, Kansas and Wisconsin vote for female suffrage.

Births

January 6—Danny Thomas, singer, actor, producer and comedian (d. 1991)

January 8—José Ferrer, Puerto Rican actor (d. 1992)

February 2—Millvina Dean, youngest passenger and survivor of the RMS *Titanic* disaster (d. 2009)

February 6—Eva Braun, Adolf Hitler's mistress (d. 1945)

March 14—Les Brown, American band leader (d. 2001)

March 16—Pat Nixon, First Lady of the United States (d. 1993)

April 2—Herbert Mills, "Mills Brothers" tenor (d. 1989)

April 8—Sonja Henie, Norwegian figure skater (d. 1969)

May 3—Virgil Fox, organist (d. 1980)

May 11—Foster Brooks, actor and comedian (d. 2001)

May 12—Archibald Cox, Watergate special prosecutor (d. 2004)

May 18—Perry Como, American singer (d. 2001)

July 14—Woody Guthrie, American folk musician ("This Land Is Your Land") (d. 1967)

July 17—Art Linkletter, American television host ("House Party') (d. 2010)

July 31—Milton Friedman, American economist and Nobel Prize laureate (d. 2006)

August 15—Julia Child, chef and author (d. 2004)

August 23—Gene Kelly, American actor (d. 1996)

September 21—Chuck Jones, American animator with Warner Brothers (d. 2002)

November 21—Eleanor Powell, American actress and dancer (d. 1982)
November 30—Gordon Parks, African American photographer and artist (d. 2006)
December 4—Gregory "Pappy" Boyington, American pilot and United States Marine Corps fighter ace (d. 1988)
December 11—Carlo Ponti, Italian film producer (d. 2007)
December 22—Lady Bird Johnson, First Lady of the United States (d. 2007)

Deaths

February 10—Joseph Lister, English surgeon (b. 1827)
April 12—Clara Barton, American nurse (b. 1821)
April 15—The following are 8 prominent names out of 1,517 victims of the RMS *Titanic* disaster:
Thomas Andrews Jr., Irish shipbuilder (b. 1873)
John Jacob Astor IV, American businessman (b. 1864)
Archibald Butt, American presidential aide (b. 1865)
Benjamin Guggenheim, American businessman (b. 1865)
Edward J. Smith, English ship captain (b. 1850)
Isidor Straus, German-born owner of Macy's (b. 1845)
Ida Straus, wife of Isidor Straus (one of only five *Titanic* first-class female fatalities) (b. 1849)
Wallace Hartley, violinist and band leader on the *Titanic* (b. 1878)
April 20—Bram Stoker, Irish writer (*Dracula*) (b. 1847)
May 30—Wilbur Wright, aviation pioneer, died of typhoid (b. 1867)
July 1—Harriet Quimby, American aviator (b. 1875)
August 20—William Booth, English founder of the Salvation Army (b. 1829)

1913 Events

January 7—William M. Burton patents a process to "crack" petroleum oil to make gasoline.
January 30—The British House of Lords rejects an Irish Home Rule Bill.
February 1—New York Grand Central Terminal, having been rebuilt, reopens as the world's largest railroad station.

February 3—The Sixteenth Amendment to the U.S. Constitution is ratified, authorizing the collection of income taxes.

March 3—The Woman Suffrage Parade of 1913 takes place in Washington, D.C., led by Inez Milholland.

March 4—Woodrow Wilson succeeds William Howard Taft as the twenty-eighth president of the United States. The U.S. Department of Commerce and U.S. Department of Labor are established. The Census Bureau, U.S. Bureau of Fisheries, the U.S. Coast and Geodetic Survey are formed as part of the Department of Commerce.

March 7—The British freighter *Alum Chine*, carrying 343 tons of dynamite, explodes in Baltimore Harbor.

March 13—Mexican revolutionary Pancho Villa returns to Mexico from his self-imposed exile in the United States.

March 18—King George I of Greece is assassinated after fifty years on the throne.

April 8—The Seventeenth Amendment to the United States Constitution is passed, dictating the direct election of senators.

April 21—Cunard ocean liner RMS *Aquitania*, built by John Brown & Company, is launched on the River Clyde.

April 26—The Panama-Pacific International Exposition opens in San Francisco.

April 29—Swedish engineer Gideon Sundback of Hoboken patents the all-purpose zipper.

May 13—Igor Sikorsky becomes the first person to pilot a four-engine aircraft.

May 14—New York governor William Sulzer approves the charter for the Rockefeller Foundation, which begins operating with a $100 million donation from John D. Rockefeller.

June 19—The Parliament of South Africa forbids blacks from owning or buying land from whites.

July 10—Death Valley, California, records 134 degrees Fahrenheit as the hottest temperature in the world as of 2013.

August 13—Stainless steel is invented by Harry Brearley in Sheffield, England.

September 9—In Germany, Badische Anilin & Soda-Fabrik (BASF) opens the world's first facility for the production of fertilizer based on the Haber-Bosch process for synthesizing ammonia. This process is still used to provide food for more than 40 percent of the world's population.

September 17—In Chicago, the Anti-Defamation League of B'nai B'rith is founded, with Sigmund Livingston as its first president.

October 10—The Gamboa Dike is opened, marking the completion of the Panama Canal construction project.

October 16—HMS *Queen Elizabeth* is launched at Portsmouth Dockyard as the first oil-fired battleship.

October 31—The Lincoln Highway, the first automobile road across the United States, is dedicated.

November 5—The builder of Castle Neuschwanstein in Germany, the insane king Ludwig II of Bavaria, is deposed by his cousin, Prince Regent Ludwig, who assumes the title Ludwig III.

November 6—Mohandas Gandhi is arrested while leading a march of Indian miners in South Africa.

November 7–11—The Great Lakes Storm, the "Freshwater Fury" of 1913, claims nineteen ships and more than 250 lives.

November 13—The first modern elastic brassiere is patented by Mary Phelps Jacob.

December 1—Henry Ford perfects the first moving assembly line, reducing chassis assembly time from twelve and a half hours to two hours and forty minutes. This ignites a new era of universal mass production.

December 12—Vincenzo Perugia tries to sell the *Mona Lisa* in Florence and is arrested.

December 23—The Federal Reserve Act creates a central banking system for the United States.

December 30—Italy returns the *Mona Lisa* to France.

Unknown date—The Camel cigarette is introduced by R.J. Reynolds in the United States, the first packaged cigarette.

Births

January 6—Loretta Young, actress (d. 2000)

January 9—Richard M. Nixon, thirty-seventh president of the United States (d. 1994)

January 15—Lloyd Bridges, actor (*Sea Hunt*) (d. 1998)

January 18– Danny Kaye, actor (d. 1987)

February 4—Rosa Parks, American civil rights activist (d. 2005); Jimmy Hoffa, labor leader (disappeared in 1975); Woody Hayes, Ohio State University football coach (d. 1987)

February 25—Jim Backus, voice actor of Mr. Magoo (d. 1989); Gert Fröbe, German actor (*Goldfinger*) (d. 1988)

March 13—William Casey, American Central Intelligence Agency director (d. 1987)
March 30—Richard Helms, American Central Intelligence Agency director (d. 2002); Frankie Laine, singer (d. 2007)
May 5—Tyrone Power, actor (d. 1958)
May 8—Bob Clampett, *Looney Tunes* director and creator of *Beanie & Cecil* (d. 1984)
May 16—Woody Herman, musician and band leader (d. 1987)
May 24—Peter Ellenshaw, artist and matte designer (*Mary Poppins*) (d. 2007)
May 26—Peter Cushing, English actor (d. 1994)
June 11—Vince Lombardi, Green Bay Packers football coach (d. 1970)
June 18—Robert Mondavi, California winemaker (d. 2008)
July 14—Gerald Ford, thirty-eighth president of the United States (d. 2006)
July 18—Red Skelton, comedian (d. 1997)
September 12—Jesse Owens, Olympic athlete and Ohio State University track star (d. 1980); Eiji Toyoda, Japanese industrialist
November 2—Burt Lancaster, American actor (*Elmer Gantry*) (d. 1994)
November 5—Vivien Leigh, British actress (*Gone with the Wind*) (d. 1967)
November 9—Hedy Lamarr, Austrian actress and inventor of frequency-hopping, which is the basis for modern spread-spectrum communication technology such as Wi-Fi and cellphones (d. 2000)

Deaths

March 10—Harriet Tubman, American abolitionist (b. 1820)
March 31—J.P. Morgan, financier and banker (b. 1837)
May 1—John Barclay Armstrong, Texas Ranger and U.S. marshal (b. 1850)
July 3—Horatio Nelson Young, Civil War naval hero (b. 1845)
July 13—Edward Burd Grubb Jr., Civil War Union brevet brigadier general (b. 1841)
September 30—Rudolf Diesel, German engine inventor (b. 1858)
December 7—Aaron Montgomery Ward, businessman and inventor of mail order (b. 1844)

Bibliography

Books and Articles

Abbett, Robert W. *American Civil Engineering Practice.* New York: John Wiley & Sons, 1956.

Alvord, John, and Charles Burdick. *Flood Protection for Columbus Ohio.* Columbus, OH: Pfeifer Press, 1913.

———. *The Franklin County Conservancy District.* Columbus, OH: New Franklin Printing, 1916.

Andersen, Douglas. *History of Dearborn and Ohio County, Indiana.* Chicago: F.E. Weakley & Company, 1885.

Andromeda, Sandy, and Leslie Blankenship. *Death and Devastation Strike Columbus Ohio.* North Liberty, OH: North Liberty Publications, 1996.

Babbitt, Harold E., and James J. Doland. *Water Supply Engineering.* New York: McGraw-Hill Book Company, 1949.

Bell Telephone News vol. 2, no. 10. "Flood Edition" (May 1913): 6–27.

Boyer, Dwight. *True Tales of the Great Lakes.* Cleveland, OH: Freshwater Press, 1971.

Brown, David G. *White Hurricane.* New York: McGraw-Hill, 2002.

Eckert, Allan W. *A Time of Terror: The Great Dayton Flood.* Dayton, OH: Landfall Press Inc., 1965.

Garrett, C.W. *History of the Flood and the Pennsylvania Rail Line.* Pittsburgh, PA: Johnston & Company Press, 1913.

Griggs, Robert F. *The Valley of Ten Thousand Smokes.* Washington, D.C.: National Geographic Society, 1922.

Hahn, Ronald. *O.W.L. Floods.* Kidron: Ohio Weather Library, 2006.

Hemming, Robert J. *Ships Gone Missing: The Great Lakes Storm of 1913.* Chicago: Contemporary Books Inc., 1992.

Hooper, Osman C. *The History of the City of Columbus.* Columbus, OH: Memorial Publishing Company, 1920.

Hutcheson, Edwin. *Floods of Johnstown: 1889, 1936, 1977.* Johnstown, PA: Cambria County Tourist Council, 1989.

Lewis, Thomas W. *Zanesville in the Flood of 1913.* Zanesville, OH: A.E. Starr Publishers, 1913.

Linsley, Ray K., and Joseph B. Franzini. *Water-Resources Engineering.* New York: McGraw-Hill Book Company, 1972.

Marshall, Logan, and L.T. Myers. *The True Story of Our National Calamity of Flood, Fire, and Tornado.* Dayton, OH: Thomas Manufacturing Company, 1913.

McCullough, David. *The Johnstown Flood.* Reprint, New York: Simon & Schuster, 1987. Originally published in 1968.

Moore, Opha. *The History of Franklin County, Ohio.* Vol. 1. Indianapolis, IN: Historical Publication Company, 1930.

Morgan, Arthur E. *Dams and Other Disasters: A Century of the Army Corps of Engineers in Civil Works.* Boston: Porter Sargent Publishing, 1971.

———. *Making of the TVA.* Buffalo, NY: Prometheus Books, 1974.

Sealander, Judith. *Grand Plans: Business Progressivism and Social Change in Ohio's Miami Valley.* Lexington: University Press of Kentucky, 1988.

Simkin, Tom, and Lee Siebert. *Volcanoes of the World.* Tucson, AZ: Geoscience Press Inc., 1994.

Simon, Andrew L. *Basic Hydraulics.* Hoboken, NJ: John Wiley & Sons, 1981.

———. *Practical Hydraulics.* Hoboken, NJ: John Wiley & Sons, 1981.

Thurber, James. *My Life and Hard Times.* New York: Harper Brothers, 1933.

Urquhart, Leonard C. *Civil Engineering Handbook.* New York: McGraw-Hill Book Company, 1959.

Williams, David J. *The History of Burgess & Niple, 1912–1992.* Cleveland, OH: Emerson Press, 1992.

NEWSPAPERS

Cleveland Plain Dealer.
Columbus Citizen Journal.
Columbus Dispatch.
Columbus Evening Dispatch.
Wheeling Intelligencer.

Index

A

air masses 53
Alvord, John W. 77
American Ship Building Company 136
American Telephone and Telegraph Company (AT&T) 93, 94
annual peak stream flow 30
Army Corps of Engineers 23
Aswan High Dam in Egypt 22
Aurora, Indiana 40
Avondale Avenue 69

B

Bell, John 93
"Big Blow" 131
Black River at Elyria 34
Broad Street 54
Buckeye Lake 61
Burdick, Charles B. 77

C

Calvary Avenue 56
cemetery coffins 83
Central Ohio Conservancy District 78
Chicago Telephone Exchange 93
Chillicothe 19, 36, 67, 105
Cincinnati 19, 34, 35
Circleville 90
Cleveland 131
Clinger, Charles 56
Columbiana County 37
Columbus city engineer 78
Columbus Evening Dispatch 51
communication 67, 93
concrete dams 118
confluence 45
Cox, Governor James 67, 96
Cuyahoga River 34, 92

D

Dana Elementary School 74
Dana Rose (baby) 74
"Day the Dam Broke, The" (Thurber short story) 84
Dayton 46, 109
Dayton, Jonathan 109
Deeds, Edward A. 126
deforestation 19
Delaware 77
Des Moines, Iowa 53

Dodridge Street Bridge 81
Dublin 77

E

Easter Sunday 41, 51

F

Fairborn, Ohio 120
Fairfield, Ohio 120
flat-bottomed boats 113
flood control 23
floodgates 65
flood of 1762 33
flood of 1832 33
flood of 1898 52
flow channel restrictions 32
Franklin Iron Works 82
Franklinton 50, 64, 96
"Freshwater Fury" 131
frozen or saturated ground 45

G

Gallipolis, Ohio 129
Gant Park 103
Garver-Quinlisk bill 119, 124
gas utilities 49
George E. Williams 78
Great Flood of 1913 41
"Great Lakes Hurricane" 131
Great Lakes ships that sank 135
Green Lawn Cemetery 58
Green, Tom 96
Griggs, Julian 84
Gyge, Paul 64

H

Hamilton 46, 47, 53, 90, 101, 108, 126
Harmon Avenue 54
Hilltop area 50
Hocking Valley Railroad 80
Hoover, Charles P. 84
Huffman Dam 120
hydrologic cycle 18
hydrologic events 29
hypothermia 69

I

Indianapolis, Indiana 19
Industrial Revolution 26
infiltration 30

J

Johnstown, Pennsylvania flood 19, 96

K

Karb, Mayor George J. 60
Kinnear, Samuel 77

L

Lake Erie 131
Lake Huron 133
La Rue, Ohio 96
Lattimer, George W. 78
Lawrenceburg, Indiana 38
levees 17, 22, 23, 32, 51, 54, 56, 58, 64, 71, 76, 79, 94, 108, 111, 118, 121, 130
Little Beaver Creek 37
Little Conemaugh River 19
Ludlow, Israel 108, 121

M

Mad River 108
Mahoning River 35
March 21 and 27 45
Marietta 34, 40, 47
May Street Cutoff 79
McKinley Avenue 54
McMahon, John 119
McMillan, William 109
Miami Canal 34
Miami Conservancy District 119
Miami River 108
Miami Valley 46
Mississippi River 23
Missouri River 42

Moore, Opha 60
Morgan, Arthur Ernest 118, 120
Mound Street 56
Mound Street Bridge 81
Mount Carmel Hospital 71
Mount Katmai 25
Mount St. Helens 26
Muncie, Indiana 94
Muskingum River 36, 49, 92

N

National Cash Register Company 113, 122
National Guard Troops 113
Native Americans 121
New Orleans 17
Newport, Kentucky 39
New Richmond 38
Niagara Falls 54
Nile River 22
North/South Poles 18, 26
Nottingham, William 133
Novarupta 25, 53, 131

O

Ohio Canal 36
Ohio Conservancy Law 119
Ohio-Erie Canal 35
Ohio River 34, 35, 40
Ohio Valley 19, 23, 24, 30, 31, 33, 34, 35, 41, 49, 53, 98
Olentangy River 50, 54, 68, 77, 78, 79, 81
Omaha, Nebraska 41
Omaha tornado 42
one-hundred-year flood 29, 30, 31
Osborn, Ohio 119
O'Shaughnessy Dam 77
Oster, Robert 64
Owen, Captain James 137

P

Parsons Avenue 85
Patterson, John H. 113, 122
Pennsylvania Railroad 49
Phoneton, Ohio 95
Pomeroy, Ohio 39
Portsmouth 38, 49, 65
Pyle, Silas 106

R

record high water 45
recurrence interval 29
Red Cross shelters 130
reestablishing telephone service 74
refugees 64, 65, 71, 74, 113
Ripley, Ohio 38
runoff 30, 50

S

Sandusky River 92
Sandusky Street 58
saturated soil 30
Scioto River 36, 46, 50, 51, 54, 57, 71, 76, 77, 80, 83, 90, 105, 130
Scioto Valley Railway 38
Sewage Pumping Station 82
sewerage facilities 49
Sexton, William 63
Shawnee tribe 108
Simpson, R.H. 78
soil erosion 19
South Fork Dam 21
spring floods 31
state capitol building 83
St. Clair, Governor Arthur 109
Steubenville 35
Stillwater River 108
Stone, Julius F. 78
stratosphere 24
streetcars 35, 42, 56, 57, 76, 117, 130, 133
sulfur aerosols 24
Sun Manufacturing Company 71
Supreme Court of Ohio 126

T

telegraph 49, 67
thunderstorms 27

Thurber, James Grover 84
Topeka, Kansas 44
Tornado Alley 28
tornados 27, 28, 41, 42, 44, 53, 98
Town Street Bridge 57
Tuscarawas River 36

U

Underwood, Charles 58
Union Depot 86
Union Telephone Company 95
U.S. Supreme Court 121

V

Volcanic Explosivity Index (VEI) 25
volcanic winter 24
Vonderheide Act 119, 125

W

Wabash River 98
Wampler, Frank 98
Watson, Thomas J. 113
Westwater, James 84
Wheeling, West Virginia 36, 38, 40, 99, 100, 101
White, Chief Justice Edward Douglass 128
White River 98
Williams, George E. 78
Wolf Creek 108
Wolfe, Robert F. 60
Wright, Orville and Wilbur 120

X

Xiaolangdi Multipurpose Dam Project 22

Y

Y-bridge in Zanesville 92, 103
Yellow (Huang He) River in China 21
Yoctangee Park 105

Z

Zanesville 19, 38, 46, 101

About the Author

Private Collection.

Conrade C. Hinds is a registered architect in Ohio and New York and a retired project manager for the City of Columbus, Division of Water. He has taught as an adjunct faculty member in the Department of Engineering Technology at Columbus State Community College for twenty-five years. Born in Nashville, Tennessee, he has lived in central Ohio for thirty-six years. As a licensed auctioneer, he likes to give back to the community by donating his services to a variety of charitable fundraising events. He is a master at yodeling, a storyteller and a historian who often incorporates the use of puppets and marionettes in his presentations. Mr. Hinds also serves on the board of the Columbus Landmarks Foundation. He is married to Dr. Janet L. Hinds, and together they have four children, Eleanor, Marshall, Serena and Nathaniel; two grandchildren, Audrey and Caleb; and a very smart dog named Porter.